Microcomputer Fault Design

Other Macmillan titles of related interest

Microcomputer Fault-finding and Design

Robin Holland

Senior Lecturer in Electronics
West Glamorgan Institute of Higher Education

MACMILLAN

First edition 1991

Published by
MACMILLAN EDUCATION LTD
Houndmills, Basingstoke, Hampshire RG21 2XS
and London
Companies and representatives
throughout the world

Printed in Hong Kong

British Library Cataloguing in Publication Data
Holland, Robin
Microcomputer fault-finding and design.
1. Microcomputer systems. Faults. Detection
I. Title
004.16
ISBN 0–333–54268–1
ISBN 0–333–54269–X pbk

Contents

Preface

Microcomputers vary from single-chip systems, such as pocket calculators, through to industrial controllers and multi-user office computers. This rapidly proliferating range of applications has brought with it a requirement for a greater understanding of this new electronic technology and for the acquisition of new skills by servicing personnel. This book is an attempt to describe the procedures and test equipment that can be applied when fault-finding on microprocessor-based equipment. There are few texts that attempt such a comprehensive coverage of this topic, and this book introduces some novel and innovative approaches to microcomputer fault detection.

Chapter 1 reviews the principles of microcomputer operation, while Chapters 2 to 8 describe items of test equipment and fault-finding procedures. The remaining chapters present a series of application studies of typical microcomputer systems which should help to give the reader an understanding of formal design procedures and servicing requirements. Appendixes describe the functions of all microprocessors and their supporting devices, while a Glossary explains the new technical vocabulary that is associated with the modern world of electronics and microcomputers.

It is assumed that the reader has an understanding of binary numbers, basic digital electronic circuits and the use of standard electronic test equipment, for example the CRO (oscilloscope). The material presented supports the maintenance topics in BTEC and City and Guilds servicing courses. Additionally, practising service engineers and technicians should find the descriptions of great benefit. Even the computer hobbyist may be able to use the procedures to locate and eliminate faults causing total system failure or partial downgrading.

Acknowledgements

The data sheets in Appendix B are reproduced, with permission, from copyright material of RS Components Ltd, Corby, Northants.

1 Microcomputer Architecture

1.1 Generalised microcomputer construction

The generalised construction of a microcomputer is illustrated in figure 1.1. The CPU (Central Processor Unit) is normally a single IC (integrated circuit) and is named the 'microprocessor'. It generates three buses, or groups of signal conductors, as follows:

(a) address bus – to select a location within a memory or input/output IC;
(b) data bus – to carry the program instruction or data item that is to be transferred in or out of the CPU;
(c) control bus – to carry control signals that activate data transfers or indicate specific events to/from the CPU.

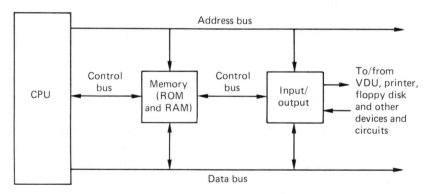

Figure 1.1 Microcomputer construction

The memory module contains the list of program instructions that is to be obeyed by the CPU, as well as data values that may be used by or generated by the CPU when it obeys the program. Memory consists normally of one or more ICs of the ROM and RAM families – to be described in section 1.4.

The input/output module passes data values into and out of the microcomputer, and connects to the following typical items of equipment:

1

(a) operator terminal, or VDU (Visual Display Unit);
(b) printer;
(c) backing store (hard disk, or floppy disk, or both) – to hold additional programs which can be transferred to memory for execution by the CPU;
(d) displays of various types, for example numerical segment displays, LED (Light Emitting Diode) indicators;
(e) data links to other computers;
(f) electrical control equipment (motors, solenoids, relays, heaters, switches);
(g) instrumentation (continuous, or 'analogue', signals);

and many others. Once again the input/output module may consist of several ICs.

Sometimes the entire circuit is contained within a single IC, for example pocket calculator, washing machine controller or telephone answering machine.

1.2   Program execution by the CPU

The CPU processes data values in groups of 8, 16 or 32 bits, where

  1 bit (binary digit) = 0 or 1

The CPU is said to have a 'word length' of 8, 16 or 32 bits. Early microcomputers and many modern microcomputers which are single-function, for example industrial sequence controllers, use 8-bit microprocessors. Office computers, for example the 'PC' (Personal Computer), possess greater computing power and employ 16-bit or 32-bit microprocessors.

The interconnecting pin functions of typical microprocessors are illustrated in figure 1.2. 8-bit microprocessors are normally mounted in 40-pin DIL (Dual-in-line) package ICs, while 16-bit and 32-bit microprocessors are held in either DIL packages of 40 to 64 pins or in 'chip carriers' (pins mounted on all four sides) of up to 120 pins. These latter packages are often called 'quad packs'.

Figure 1.3 shows the principal modules within the CPU and the way in which it connects to a memory IC that contains the program that it is to obey. Memory locations are 8-bits ('byte') wide, and the program for this 8-bit microprocessor is shown in 'machine code, that is the bit pattern that is held in each memory location. Notice that this bit pattern is shown in the abbreviated hex (hexadecimal) form, for example

  hex 3E = 0011 1110 in binary

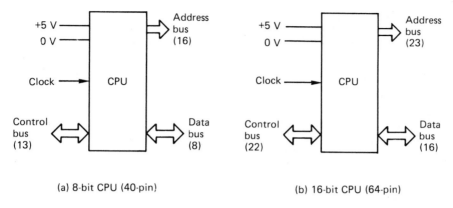

(a) 8-bit CPU (40-pin) (b) 16-bit CPU (64-pin)

Figure 1.2 CPU pin functions

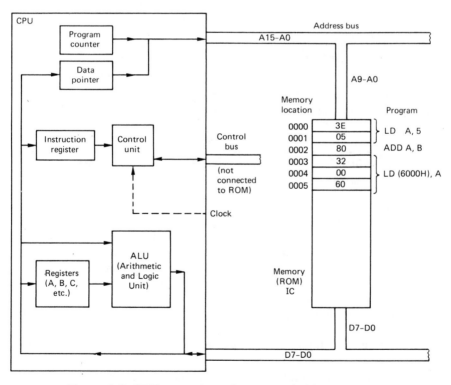

Figure 1.3 CPU execution of program held in memory

Table 1.1 shows the binary to hexadecimal character relationship.

Table 1.1 Binary to hexadecimal conversion

Binary	Hexadecimal
0000	0
0001	1
0010	2
0011	3
0100	4
0101	5
0110	6
0111	7
1000	8
1001	9
1010	A
1011	B
1100	C
1101	D
1110	E
1111	F

The first three instructions in the program are shown in figure 1.3, and are fully documented in the following way:

Memory address (hex)	Machine code (hex)	Assembly language (mnemonic form)	Comments
0000	3E,05	LD A,5	Load A register with 5
0002	80	ADD A,B	Add B register to A register
0003	32,00,60	LD (6000H),A	Store A register into memory location 6000

Notice that instructions are of variable length (1, 2 or 3 bytes) for this 8-bit microprocessor, for example the Zilog Z80. Each instruction is obeyed by the CPU using the 'fetch–execute' cycle, as follows:

(a) fetch – the instruction byte (called 'opcode') is fetched from memory;
(b) execute – the opcode, which is held within the CPU's instruction register, is obeyed by the CPU; this frequently involves reading one or more bytes (the 'operand') out of memory into the CPU.

The roles of the CPU's individual modules can be summarised as follows:

(1) *Instruction register* – holds the opcode while the CPU obeys each instruction.
(2) *Control unit* – examines the opcode, and sends signals around the CPU, and beyond the CPU (on the control bus), in order to implement the instruction; each action that it performs is triggered by a pulse on the Clock signal.
(3) *Registers* – hold data items processed by the program.
(4) *ALU* – performs arithmetic (add, subtract, etc.) and logic (AND, OR, etc.) on data items.
(5) *Program counter* – holds the memory address of the next program instruction word that is to be read from memory.
(6) *Data pointer* – holds the memory address of a data item to be read from, or written to, memory.

The sequence of events that occurs when the CPU obeys the three program instructions in this example is illustrated in figure 1.4. The CPU steps through memory locations consecutively, unless a 'jump' instruction is encountered. This redirects the CPU to a different memory location – the program counter is loaded with this new memory address. Every program terminates with a jump instruction. Occasionally an 'input/output' instruction is encountered, and this transfers a data item through an input/output IC.

Although this program example is based on an 8-bit CPU, the same principles of operation apply to 16-bit CPUs. Normally the instruction opcode is two bytes long (occupies two memory locations), and data items similarly are two bytes in length. Clearly this can be extended for 32-bit CPUs.

Although none of the control bus lines were utilised in this simple example, they are applied in full circuit configurations, and the most important and commonly encountered control bus signals are as follows.

(a) Interrupts, frequently named:

RESET – when set this forces the CPU's program counter to a fixed value (typically 0000);

NMI (Non-Maskable Interrupt) – forces the program counter to a different memory address, which contains the start of the 'interrupt service routine' which is activated by the setting of the interrupt signal;

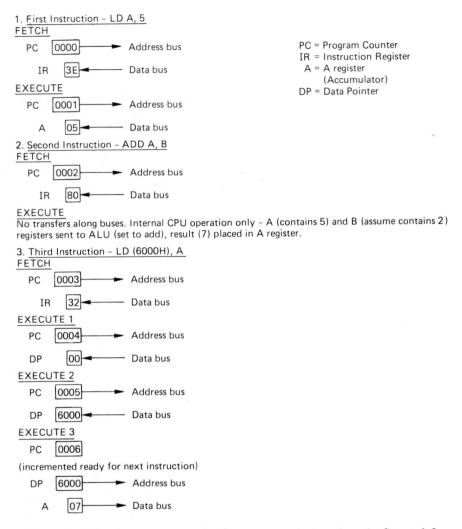

1. First Instruction - LD A, 5
FETCH

   PC   0000 ⟶ Address bus

   IR   3E ⟵ Data bus

EXECUTE

   PC   0001 ⟶ Address bus

   A   05 ⟵ Data bus

PC = Program Counter
IR = Instruction Register
A = A register
    (Accumulator)
DP = Data Pointer

2. Second Instruction - ADD A, B
FETCH

   PC   0002 ⟶ Address bus

   IR   80 ⟵ Data bus

EXECUTE
No transfers along buses. Internal CPU operation only - A (contains 5) and B (assume contains 2) registers sent to ALU (set to add), result (7) placed in A register.

3. Third Instruction - LD (6000H), A
FETCH

   PC   0003 ⟶ Address bus

   IR   32 ⟵ Data bus

EXECUTE 1

   PC   0004 ⟶ Address bus

   DP   00 ⟵ Data bus

EXECUTE 2

   PC   0005 ⟶ Address bus

   DP   6000 ⟵ Data bus

EXECUTE 3

   PC   0006

(incremented ready for next instruction)

   DP   6000 ⟶ Address bus

   A   07 ⟶ Data bus

Figure 1.4 Fetch – execute cycles for program instructions in figure 1.3

    INT – different techniques are applied to cause the CPU to commence obeying a servicing interrupt program (interrupt service routine).

There may be more than three interrupt signals.

(b) Read (for example RD) – selects direction of data transfer in or out of memory or input/output along the bi-directional data bus.
(c) Write (for example WR) – inverse of (b).

(d) Memory Request (for example MREQ) – selects memory ICs.
(e) Input/Output Request (for example IORQ) – selects input/output ICs.
(f) Direct Memory Access (DMA) Request and Acknowledge (for example BUSRQ and BUSAK, or HOLD and HOLDA) – an input/output IC uses these handshaking signals to ask the CPU to disconnect itself from the buses such that it can address memory ICs itself using the CPU's buses.

1.3 Address decoding

A microprocessor with 16 address bus lines can address:

$$2^{16} = 64K \ (65\ 536)\ \text{memory locations} \qquad 1K = 1024$$

Similarly a CPU with 23 address bus lines can address:

$$2^{23} = 8M\ \text{memory locations} \qquad 1M = 1K \times 1K$$

The memory ICs must fit into different sections of this 'memory map', and a circuit arrangement must be made to ensure that only one IC is selected at a time. Figure 1.5(a) illustrates how an address decoder IC is used to perform this function. Two memory ICs (ROM devices – to be described in the next section) connect to the address and data buses in an identical manner, but each receives a different CE (Chip Enable) – sometimes called CS (Chip Select) – from an address decoder circuit. This circuit ensures that only one CE signal can be set at a time – the signal is set low (0 V), as indicated in the figure by the bar above the CE legend and by the bubble at the output connection of the address decoder and the input connection to the ROM. Thus only one memory IC can be selected at any time. The address decoder IC must itself be activated by the setting of the G (Enable) signal, and this is commonly connected to the CPU's control bus signal MREQ (Memory Request). Notice that there are two spare unused CE signals in this particular arrangement.

ROM1 possesses 2048 memory locations as follows:

$$11\ \text{address lines give } 2^{11} = 2048\ \text{addressable locations}$$

and each location holds 8 bits (8 data bus connections). Its 'memory organisation' is therefore said to be

$$2048 \times 8$$

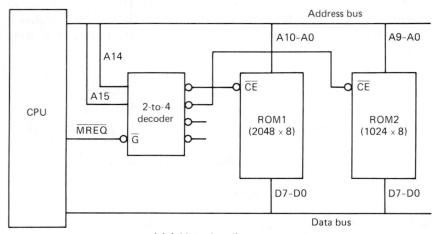

(a) Address decoding arrangement

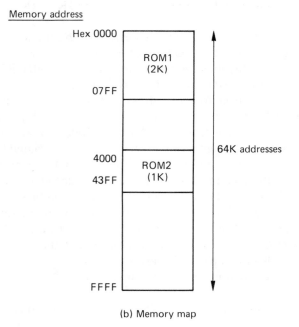

(b) Memory map

Figure 1.5 Microcomputer memory circuit

Similarly ROM2 is

$$1024 \times 8$$

The operation of the address decoder IC can be summarised by the 'truth table' shown in table 1.2.

Table 1.2 *Truth table for 2 to 4
decoder (SN74LS139 IC)*

A15	A14	$\overline{CE4}$	$\overline{CE3}$	$\overline{CE2}$	$\overline{CE1}$
0	0	1	1	1	0
0	1	1	1	0	1
1	0	1	0	1	1
1	1	0	1	1	1

From this table the memory addresses of the two ROMs in figure 1.5(a) can be calculated as shown in table 1.3. Notice that unused inputs are shown as 'X' and are assumed to be 0. The memory ranges of each IC can then be summarised in the 'memory map' of figure 1.5(b).

Table 1.3   *Address calculations for figure 1.5*

Hex.	Address line (An)																
	15	14	13	12	11	10	9	8	7	6	5	4	3	2	1	0	
0000	0	0	X	X	X	0	0	0	0	0	0	0	0	0	0	0	ROM1 start
07FF	0	0	X	X	X	1	1	1	1	1	1	1	1	1	1	1	ROM1 end
4000	0	1	X	X	X	X	0	0	0	0	0	0	0	0	0	0	ROM2 start
43FF	0	1	X	X	X	X	1	1	1	1	1	1	1	1	1	1	ROM2 end

$\longleftrightarrow$

$$\begin{bmatrix} \text{Address} \\ \text{decoder} \end{bmatrix}$$

Address decoding circuit arrangements for input/output ICs are the same as for memory devices. The reader may like to repeat the above analysis for the input/output circuit shown in figure 1.6(a). The principle of operation of a 3-to-8 decoder is the same as for a 2-to-4 decoder – an increasing binary count on the inputs sets each consecutive output signal in order to select a different input/output IC. Notice that only one-half of the address bus (A7–A0) is used for input/output addressing in this case because of the smaller number of addressable locations (4 in this example) within input/output ICs. The reader should produce the input/output map of figure 1.6(b).

Although analysed separately here, the memory and input/output circuits of figures 1.5 and 1.6 are typically combined to produce a full microcomputer circuit. Several microprocessors do not possess input/

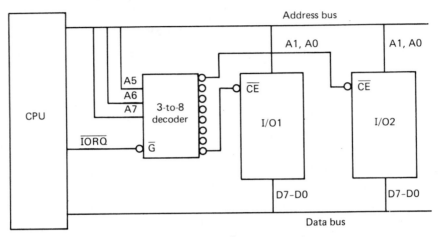

(a) Address decoding arrangement

Input/output addresses

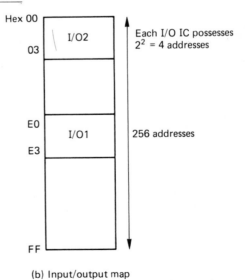

(b) Input/output map

Figure 1.6 Microcomputer input/output circuit

output program instructions, and therefore do not distinguish between memory and input/output ICs. In this arrangement the two types of device connect to the address and data buses as before, but receive their CE signals from the same address decoder circuit, for example a 3-to-8 decoder, and input/output is described as being 'memory mapped'.

1.4 Memory ICs

Memory ICs are either

(a) ROM – Read-Only Memory, or
(b) RAM – Read/write memory (RAM = Random Access Memory).

ROM can be subdivided into:

(1) ROM – Programmed when IC is designed and manufactured;
(2) PROM – Programmable ROM, programmed by user;
(3) EPROM – Erasable PROM, can be re-programmed many times.

Normally members of this ROM family are pin-compatible, so that a circuit board is designed and tested using EPROM devices because of their re-programmable nature, but then manufactured in larger numbers using cheaper ROM devices. A UV (ultra-violet) light source is required to erase EPROMs.

Every computer will hold part or all of its program in ROM rather than RAM, so that on switch-on this program will be entered – see RESET in section 1.2. This is because the apparent read/write advantage of RAM is offset by its 'volatility', that is it loses its stored bit pattern when dc power is removed (for example when the machine is switched off). However most microcomputers possess some RAM, and in disk-based machines most programs are held on disk and transferred down into RAM when they are to be executed. Additionally, data items can only be stored temporarily into RAM of course.

As with ROM, RAM can also be subdivided, as follows:

(1) static RAM;
(2) dynamic RAM – volatile in the same manner as static RAM, but also requires a 'refresh' operation more frequently than once every 2 ms (typically) to prevent loss of stored bit pattern.

Figure 1.7 illustrates a typical microcomputer memory circuit. ROM and RAM (static) devices possess the same pin functions, with the addition in the case of RAM of a Read/Write (named WR in this example) signal to

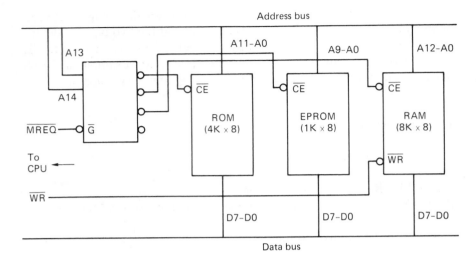

Figure 1.7 Memory circuit

select the direction of data transfer. The reader may like to further test his/her understanding of address decoding to calculate the address ranges of these memory devices. The answers should be:

ROM start   : 0000 (hex)
ROM end   : 0FFF
EPROM start : 2000
EPROM end   : 23FF
RAM start   : 4000
RAM end   : 5FFF

Large RAM systems, for example 8K bytes up to 1M or more, use dynamic RAM in place of static RAM because of cost considerations. The much reduced cost of dynamic RAM ICs compared with static RAM outweighs the cost of the additional circuitry that is required for dynamic RAM arrays. Figure 1.8 illustrates the way in which 16 384 × 1 dynamic RAM ICs are connected to provide 64K bytes of storage. The dynamic RAM controller IC performs the following functions:

(a) Generates 4 Chip Select signals (decodes A15 and A14 to produce RAS0, RAS1, RAS2 and RAS3) – each RAS signal selects one 16K bank of memory made up of 8 separate 16K × 1 4116 dynamic RAM ICs.
(b) Generates the CAS signal, which indicates that either A6–A0 (firstly) or A13–A7 (secondly) address bus signals are placed on the shared (multiplexed) A6–A0 pins on all dynamic RAM ICs. This address

signal multiplexing is applied to reduce the number of interconnecting pins on the RAM ICs, thus reducing size and cost.

(c) Generates a refresh count, which is placed on the address pins of each RAM when it is not addressed by the address bus. This is the technique of refreshing dynamic RAM faster than every 2 ms to ensure that the stored bit pattern is not lost.

The de-multiplexing ICs are required to split the bi-directional data bus into separate uni-directional data in and data out signals. This is because each dynamic RAM IC in this arrangement has a separate data in and data out signal pin. Notice that each RAM device stores only one bit, and so each IC connects to a different data bus line, for example the left-hand IC stores D7 and the right-hand IC stores D0.

For simplicity, the other three banks, each of 8 dynamic RAM ICs, are not shown.

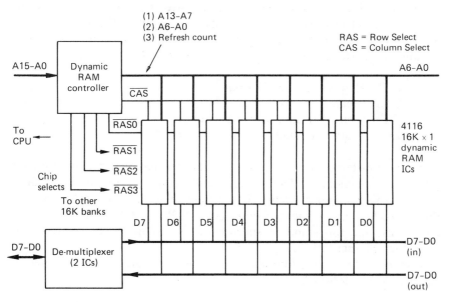

Figure 1.8 Dynamic RAM system (64 bytes)

1.5 Input/output ICs

A range of 'intelligent' input/output ICs is available to enable each microprocessor type to connect to external devices and systems. The most common devices are:

(a) PIO (Parallel Input/Output) – connects 8 parallel data bits through 'ports' to such devices as printers, segment displays and pushbuttons.
(b) UART (Universal Asynchronous Receiver Transmitter) – connects 8 data bits in serial, both out and in, to remote serial-drive peripherals, for example VDU or data link to another computer.
(c) CTC (Counter Timer Circuit) – a programmable counter.
(d) FDC (Floppy Disk Controller) – controls the drive circuitry to two (normally) floppy disk units.
(e) CRT (Cathode Ray Tube) controller – generates a video signal for connection to a CRT to produce alphanumeric character displays.
(f) DMA (Direct Memory Access) controller – allows an FDC or CRT controller to access memory directly.

The first three devices are illustrated in figure 1.9. The CTC is required to generate an accurate clock signal to the UART. The CTC simply divides an incoming high-frequency signal (normally the CPU clock) by a binary count to produce a lower-frequency pulse stream. The UART uses this clock signal to trigger the transfer of bits serially out on the Tx pin, and in on the Rx pin. The UART uses two pairs of handshaking control signals to communicate with the remote peripheral, as follows:

RTS (Request To Send) – out $\left.\right\}$ Pair 1
CTS (Clear To Send)   – in
DTR (Data Terminal Ready) – out $\left.\right\}$ Pair 2
DSR (Data Set Ready)   – in

Data are transferred in byte form using the international ASCII character set – see Appendix C. The waveform of each transmitted character is described in Chapter 5 (figure 5.4), where faults in serial data links are discussed. Similarly Chapter 5 describes the 'RS232-C' standard for serial data links, and this standard specifies transmission speeds (bits/second) and other characteristics.

Most UARTS possess four addressable registers (selected by settings on A0 and A1) as follows:

Tx (transmit data)– 0
Rx (receive data) – 1
Control register   – 2
Status register   – 3

A control byte must initially be set into the control register by the drive program to select the programmable RS232-C options. The status register holds 'flags' which are set by the UART to indicate its internal state, for example transmit character cleared, character received.

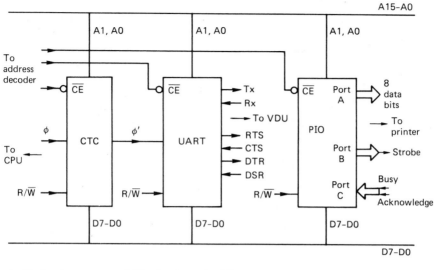

φ = Clock pulse   R/W̄ = Read/Write (or W̄R̄)

Figure 1.9 Input/output circuit for VDU and printer

The PIO passes data out and in via 8-bit parallel 'ports'. PIOs possess either two or three ports. In figure 1.9 only one bit of Port B and two bits of Port C are utilised for handshaking control signals for the parallel 'Centronics' interface to a printer. The port directions are 'programmable', that is they are selected by the control program setting a control byte into the addressable 'control register'. The addresses within a PIO are typically

> Port A – 0
> Port B – 1
> Port C – 2
> Control register – 3

as selected by the address bit settings on A1 and A0. Some PIOs possess a CTC circuit additionally, thus avoiding the requirement for a separate CTC IC when a programmable counter is required. Frequently PIO ports are employed in a multiplexed arrangement (different signals pass along common conductors) when large numbers of signals are handled, as shown in figure 1.10. In example (a) a keyboard of 64 pushbuttons is arranged in a matrix, so that the 8 input signal lines are shared by 8 columns of 8 pushbuttons each – a contact-closure pushbutton is connected between each column and row line. The control program sets the top signal on Port A firstly, and the right-hand column of pushbuttons is read in through Port B to determine if any key is pressed. This is then repeated for the

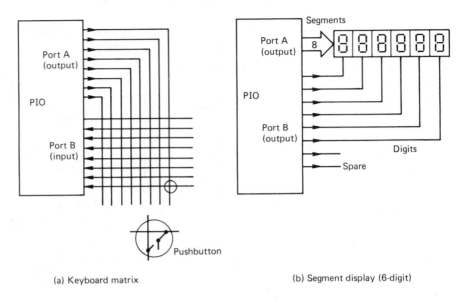

(a) Keyboard matrix   (b) Segment display (6-digit)

Figure 1.10 PIO multiplexed ports

succeeding Port A (column) signals. In this way only 2 ports are required to read in 64 signals, instead of 8 ports if multiplexing is not used. In example (b) Port A drives 8 segment signals that are commoned (or 'bussed') to all 6 display units. The bit pattern output to Port B selects which of the 6 display units is to display that segment pattern. The control program must refresh each display unit (with segment pattern and digit select) repetitively to refresh the display system – each unit is illuminated for one-sixth of the total time. Once again this multiplexing arrangement reduces the number of ports required (from 6 to 2).

If the programmable feature of PIO port direction setting is not required, simple 8-bit buffer ICs (TTL devices) can be used in place of PIOs – Appendix B lists the functions of the TTL (Transistor Transistor Logic) range of ICs. Notice that all ICs described previously in this chapter are VLSI (Very Large Scale Integration) devices manufactured using MOS (Metal Oxide Semiconductor) fabrication technology.

The use of the other three input/output ICs (FDC, CRT controller and DMA controller) mentioned at the beginning of this section is illustrated in Appendix A (Intel 8085 and Motorola 6809 data sheets). A CRT controller generates a video signal in order to display alphanumeric characters in the following manner:

(a) ASCII characters are removed from the microcomputer's main memory (RAM) to produce a dot matrix pattern for application to the video connection to a CRT – as applied in PCs (Personal Computers) and home computers.

(b) The same arrangement is applied in a VDU (computer terminal), which is itself microprocessor-based normally and is connected by RS232-C data link to the remote computer, except that characters are removed from the VDU's RAM (typically 2K for 80 characters × 24 rows), which is filled when characters are received along the serial link.

Examination of the Intel 8085 data sheet illustrates the way in which this common circuit arrangement operates:

(1) The CRT controller requests a DMA transfer (sets DRQ2); DMA controller acknowledges by setting DACK2.
(2) DMA controller requests control of the microcomputer's buses – sets HOLD; CPU responds by setting HOLDA and 'floating' its buses.
(3) DMA controller sets memory address of character to be displayed.
(4) CRT controller receives ASCII character from RAM, and uses this code to address Character Generator ROM to produce top row of dots in dot matrix pattern for that character – the Line Counter 4 bits are set to zero for this first row.

This procedure is repeated for the top dot matrix row for all 80 (typically) characters, and then repeated for each other dot matrix row (with a different value set on the Line Counter 4 bits), until the first row of 80 characters is constructed. This whole cycle is then repeated for each of the other 23 (typically) rows of characters.

Floppy-disk transfers can occur in a similar way using DMA. The operation of an FDC is described in detail in section 5.4.

1.6 Stack

Most microcomputers set aside a small area of RAM for use as a 'stack'. The stack is used to store the return address when a program calls a subroutine. A subroutine is a section of program that is normally placed after the main program in memory, and it is utilised (called) more than once by the main program. Therefore the overall program length is reduced, thus saving memory space.

Figure 1.11 illustrates how a CPU register (the Stack Pointer) holds the memory address of the last used location on the stack. When an instruction in the main program calls the subroutine, program control is transferred to the start of the subroutine, and the CPU automatically stores the return address on the stack; the stack pointer is adjusted. When the RETURN instruction is obeyed the CPU removes the return address from the stack,

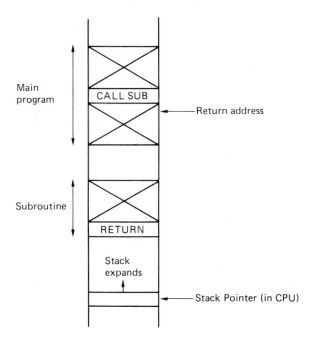

Figure 1.11 Stack mechanism

places it in the Program Counter in the CPU (see figure 1.3) and transfers program control back to the instruction that followed the CALL instruction; the Stack Pointer is adjusted back to its original setting. The subroutine can call another subroutine, such that two return addresses are stacked on top of each other in the stack area.

The stack can also be used to store the contents of CPU registers (for example A, B, C, etc.) when entering a subroutine. This is performed to prevent the subroutine overwriting data values that are being processed by the main program. Normally this is carried out at the beginning of the subroutine using PUSH instructions (for example PUSH BC stores B and C registers on the stack on top of the return address). The CPU registers are then reinstated off the stack to the end of the subroutine using POP instructions (for example POP BC).

The stack mechanism of storing return addresses automatically is also used by an interrupt program (or ISR – Interrupt Service Routine), which is entered when an interrupt signal is set.

1.7 Co-processors

Most 16-bit and 32-bit microprocessor manufacturers offer co-processors to support the CPU to perform some of its functions faster. These devices simply connect to the CPU's buses, as shown in figure 1.12, and monitor activity until they are triggered to perform their circuit function. The two types of co-processors that are commonly encountered are:

(a) Numeric co-processor – this performs hardware floating point operations, for example adds two 64-bit numbers expressed in floating point form (multi-byte representation to hold large and fractional numbers), and other high-resolution integer and trigonometric functions.
(b) Input/output co-processor – this performs block data transfers (typically using DMA) between CPU and peripherals (for example backing store).

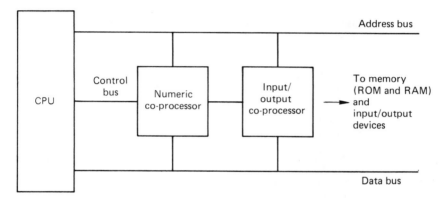

Figure 1.12 Co-processors

Bibliography

1. R. C. Holland, *Microprocessors and their Operating Systems*, Pergamon, 1989.
2. R. C. Holland, *Integrated Circuits and Microprocessors*, Pergamon, 1986.

2   Testing an Unresponsive Computer

2.1   Introduction

An unresponsive computer is one that does not communicate with the operator through the normal operator display device, for example VDU (terminal) or numerical display. When switched on the computer appears to be 'dead', for example

(a) an office computer (or home computer) produces a blank CRT display;
(b) an industrial control computer does not respond to manual or automatic signal stimulus;
(c) a microcomputer system in the form of a microprocessor-based peripheral, for example printer or VDU, is totally inactive.

Although a computer is a far more complicated electronic system than conventional domestic electronic devices and industrial control or logging systems, servicing and fault-finding is not necessarily much more specialised or complicated. The same types of fault predominate with computers as with other systems, for example power supply failure, electromechanical unreliability, observably damaged components, interconnector faults, etc. The service engineer who has experience with TV (and similar) repairs can use many of his skills when adapting to computer maintenance.

2.2   Power supply checks

Let us assume that we are dealing with a typical fault with an office computer that does not produce a 'prompt' on the screen when the machine is switched on. Firstly, confirm the following:

(a) Is the machine switched on?
(b) Is the machine receiving power? Most computers will have an indicator LED. Alternatively, the cooling fan may not be rotating.
(c) If there is no power reaching the machine, the plug and fuse should be checked.

An analogue or digital multimeter (for example DVM) is required for the following checks. Examine the ac input voltage, which normally should be 240 V – a blown fuse is the probable cause of a 0 V reading (*Note:* beware of the danger of electrical shock when testing ac mains voltages.) Examine the dc voltage out of the power supply unit to the circuit board/boards. This should be +5 V, although frequently other dc rail voltage levels are also required. Figure 2.1 illustrates the typical arrangement for a +5 V dc power supply, together with normal voltage levels. Typical faults that can occur are:

(a) Blown fuse.
(b) Damaged winding in the transformer – frequently the distinctive 'fish' smell of a burnt electrical winding is an obvious indication of this fault. If the transformer is isolated from the circuit, a continuity check on the primary and secondary windings can be made – a dc resistance of an ohm or less is normal.
(c) A faulty bridge rectifier (normally a single 4-pin component) is a frequent cause of a 0 V dc output voltage reading.
(d) The dc regulator, which normally dissipates several watts of power and consequently runs very hot, can fail open-circuit or short-circuit. The latter produces a high dc output voltage level, which can occasionally damage circuit components.
(e) A smoothing capacitor could go 'leaky', that is short-circuit, producing a low dc voltage output level, or open-circuit, in which case dc regulation will be poor. In this latter case, the unwanted ripple on the dc voltage rail will almost certainly inhibit circuit operation. Measurement by a CRO indicates whether ripple is present.

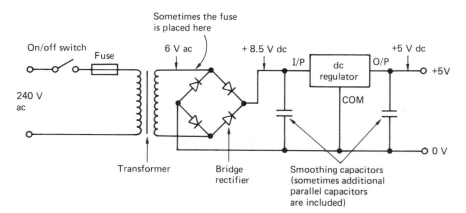

Figure 2.1 Normal dc power supply circuit (for +5 V and 0 V)

It should be noted that low dc power levels, for example 4.5 V, can give the unusual effect of not affecting MOS devices, for example microprocessor, RAM, ROM and programmable input/output devices, but will cause TTL devices to malfunction. This is because TTL is less tolerant of incorrect dc rail voltages.

If the dc rail voltage level is low, it should not be automatically assumed that the power supply is faulty. It may be that the circuit load is too great for the design capacity of the power supply, for example a short-circuit between positive and negative rails may have occurred, thus dragging the dc output voltage low. In this case the power supply should be disconnected from its load (the circuit board/boards), and then its output voltage should be re-measured.

A simple test that does not require any test equipment to confirm that the +5 V dc supply has failed is to touch each of the main ICs in the circuit board several minutes after the machine has been switched on. If they appear cold to the touch then almost certainly they are not receiving the +5 V supply. Indeed this test can be carried further, and the location of the loss of the +5 V distribution around a board can be identified – perhaps a decoupling capacitor across the +5 V and Ground terminals of an IC has gone short-circuit.

Some circuit components require +12 V and −12 V dc power supply levels, for example some EPROMs and an RS232-C serial interface circuit. In this case separate windings and rectifier/regulator circuits are required within the power supply in order to generate these additional dc power levels.

A variation of the traditional power supply circuit discussed above is the switched mode power supply. Such power supplies are often used for computer systems which present high loads, for example +5 V at 10 A or more. The advantage offered is that the transformer (which operates at high frequency rather than 50 Hz mains frequency) is much smaller. Additionally the power supply is more efficient. The basic operation of a switched mode power supply is illustrated in figure 2.2.

Some low-power (electrical and computing) home computers have their mains transformer removed from the equipment housing and mounted within the mains plug. The input to the equipment box is then typically 9 V ac.

A useful alternative to a multimeter to confirm the presence of +5 V dc level is a LED indicator, as illustrated in figure 2.3. In (a) the LED is illuminated at variable intensities, depending on the dc voltage level. In (b) the LED does not illuminate at all when the dc voltage level is less than +3 V, because the zener breakdown voltage is not exceeded and no conduction occurs.

Occasionally a mains supply filter is provided to eliminate switching transients initiated by adjacent equipment from the mains supply to the

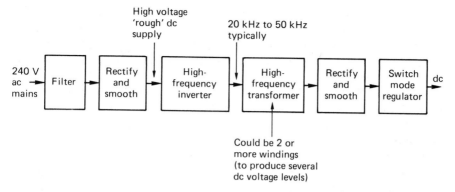

Figure 2.2 Switch mode power supply

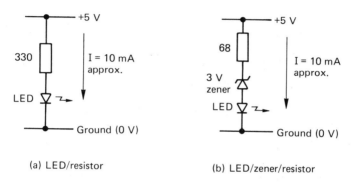

(a) LED/resistor   (b) LED/zener/resistor

Figure 2.3 LED indicator circuit for TTL logic levels

computer. Sometimes the filter is built into the mains plug itself. Clearly, failure of this filter/suppressor should be checked in the event of loss of ac supply.

Most computers possess a RESET button. When pressed the main program is re-entered (it may have to be automatically loaded down from backing store). Some home computers require to be switched off and then on again to perform the same function. Clearly, if the computer appears to be inoperative this is a sensible procedure to implement before a fault is presumed.

2.3   Initial CRO checks

A CRO, or 'oscilloscope', is an extremely useful item of test equipment to apply to fault-finding on computers and other electronic systems. Although its primary function is to display ac and pulse waveforms, it can also indicate dc levels, and therefore can be used to test dc voltages in power supplies as described in the previous section. However the inherent visual inaccuracy of dc measurement using a CRO compared with a DVM should be remembered.

Before a CRO is used to monitor test points around a computer circuit, it is sensible to make a careful visual examination of the computer circuit board/boards. Frequently faults are readily apparent, for example damaged component (signs of overheating – black IC package partly discoloured to grey), broken component wire, plug/socket not firmly connected, broken copper track, IC not firmly fixed into socket, short-circuit across copper tracks or component connections. Poor connections at some point in the system can often be aggravated or temporarily cleared by physically flexing or jolting the board or overall system.

The following checks with a CRO can be performed quickly and simply:

(a) Check the dc supply to the main ICs.
(b) Confirm that there is bus activity on the address and data buses. Normally the CPU repeatedly obeys program instructions in memory, that is it continuously implements the fetch–execute cycle. In this case, pulse activity on the address and data buses will be continuous. It is virtually impossible to synchronise the CRO to these relatively random waveforms, but at least an active CPU can be confirmed. Notice that the 'floating' state is indicated on a data bus line using a CRO by an intermediate voltage level between 0 V and +5 V – the data bus should be held in the floating state for approximately 50 per cent of the overall time when the CPU is executing a program. If there is not activity on the address and data buses, proceed to the following tests.
(c) The CPU clock input should be examined – without it the CPU will not step through its fetch – execute cycle. Figure 2.4 shows a typical TTL clock generator circuit that is connected to the clock pin on the CPU. Sometimes the quartz crystal and the capacitor are interchanged. The clock frequency (and even the voltage level) should be checked. Some microprocessors provide their own clock generator circuits on-chip, but they still require the connection of a crystal to stabilise the frequency of oscillation. A CPU will normally operate successfully with some reduction in clock frequency, but rarely for an increase in clock frequency. Sometimes a crystal will break into an overtone, thus increasing the clock speed. Suspect crystals should be unsoldered carefully to avoid damage. Some microprocessors require two clock inputs (for example the 6502), and so both should be checked.
(d) Interrupts (including the power-up RESET) can become permanently set, and thus cause the CPU to lock into the RESET state or continuously attempt to service a phantom interrupt. Consider the

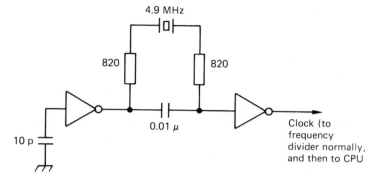

Figure 2.4 CPU clock circuit

normal RESET circuit of figure 2.5. The *RC* time constant is long
enough to ensure that the CPU is held in the RESET state for sufficient
time to allow its internal registers to be initialised correctly, for
example the program counter is set to 0 on most microprocessors.
Correct functioning of this circuit can be tested by pressing the RESET
pushbutton, or switching the computer off and on, while monitoring
the RESET pin on the CPU with a CRO. The operation of the RESET
pushbutton can be duplicated by the temporary connection of a length
of wire across the capacitor. An interruption of the mains supply, or a
temporary glitch on the RESET line, can cause unwanted system
resets. In a similar way, incorrect setting of an interrupt line, for
example NMI (Non-maskable Interrupt) or INT (maskable interrupt),
can cause erroneous program execution by the CPU. The CPU may

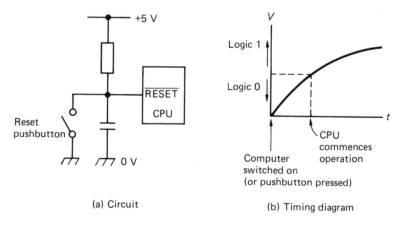

(a) Circuit   (b) Timing diagram

Figure 2.5 CPU reset circuit

spend most of its time attempting to service the interrupt, and if the interrupt line is not actually used in a particular application, there may in fact not be an interrupt program established in memory for it. The use of a CRO might highlight the fact that an interrupt line is set (invariably interrupts are set at the 0 V level) when it should not be.

(e) The DMA (Direct Memory Access) control signals should be checked with a CRO for an inoperative CPU. These handshaking lines are called typically HOLD (DMA Request – from an input/output device) and HOLDA (DMA Acknowledge – set by the CPU in response to HOLD). The setting of HOLD (normally to the 0 V level) causes the CPU to float its buses so that an input/output device can use the buses to access memory directly. Therefore the incorrect (perhaps permanent) setting of HOLD can cause the CPU to enter a state of suspension. Alternatively if CRO measurements show the data bus, address bus and some of the control bus lines (for example Read/Write and IO/Memory, or equivalent) are permanently in the floating state, then the incorrect setting of HOLD should be suspected.

(f) It may be profitable to check additional control bus lines which may help to indicate the cause of an inactive CPU. Some CPUs generate secondary clock signals, or other signals which indicate the internal state of the CPU.

(g) One final check with a CRO may be useful. The circuit should be examined to determine if there are any buffers on the address and data buses before they are distributed to the memory and input/output circuits. If buffers are present the outputs should be examined for activity – the same types of waveforms as described in (b) should be observed, of course. Additionally the address decoding circuit could be examined, and activity on the CS (Chip Select) signals to the main memory chips (particularly the ROM/PROM/EPROM that contains the start-up program entered on RESET) should be confirmed.

2.4   NOP (No-operation) test

A NOP (or 'free-run') test is designed to test the 'kernel' of a computer, that is the CPU and its surrounding circuitry only. The CPU is forced to obey a dummy instruction repetitively, and correct operation of the kernel can be confirmed by monitoring address bus lines with a CRO.

The kernel comprises the CPU itself, the clock generator circuit, the address bus (perhaps including any buffers) and of course the power supply. The NOP test free-runs the CPU by clamping a fixed instruction permanently on to the data bus. This instruction must be a single-byte instruction for an 8-bit microprocessor, and the most common instruction chosen is the NOP (No-operation) instruction. When the computer is switched on therefore, the CPU attempts to fetch–execute instructions from consecutive memory locations (normally starting at location 0), but each opcode it sees is the free-run, or no-operation instruction. It therefore continually obeys this instruction, but steps through each memory location from 0000 to FFFF (for an 8-bit microprocessor), and then repeats the cycle – after FFFF the program counter increments to 0000. The waveforms observed on a CRO for each address bus line should therefore be as shown in figure 2.6. Address bus line A0 should change at the highest frequency (typically 500 kHz), A1 at half this frequency, and so on. Additionally, relevant control bus lines can be checked, for example Read/Write.

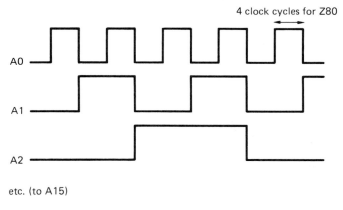

Figure 2.6 Address bus waveforms for NOP test

When a microprocessor circuit board is designed it is possible to build in a set of switches into the data bus connections from the CPU, so that a free-run instruction can be forced on to the data bus by simply setting switches. Figure 2.7 shows the arrangement for a Z80 microprocessor. If S1 (8-way) is opened and S2 is closed, the opcode 7F (a single-byte instruction – LD A, A) is forced on to the data pins of the CPU. The CPU will then cycle through memory continuously. Normally the LD A,A instruction is chosen in place of the NOP instruction because the opcode is easier to generate with switches.

It is rare to find a CPU board that contains such a facility, and so it is necessary to devise an arrangement whereby a free-run instruction can be introduced into the data bus connections without having to resort to cutting copper tracks, or some other inconvenient measure. A practical solution is shown in figure 2.8, again for a Z80 microprocessor. The CPU is removed from its socket in the board under test, and placed into a double wire-wrap socket arrangement which connects 32 of the 40 pins of the CPU straight through into the circuit board. The 8 data bus connections are intercepted,

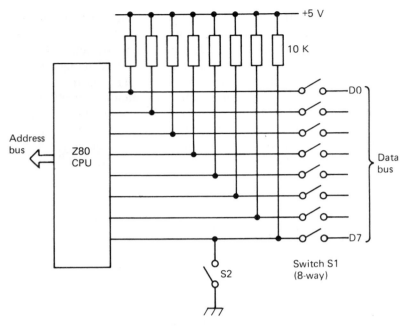

Figure 2.7 data bus switches for Z80 free-run test (using LD A, A – 7F)

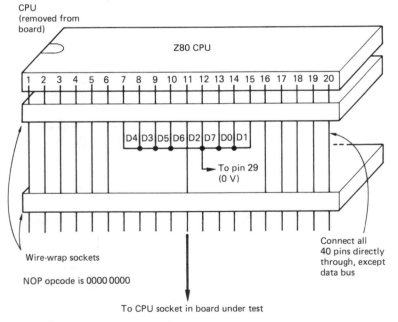

Figure 2.8 Free-run connector for Z80 CPU (using NOP – 00)

and are all connected to the 0 V pin. In this way an opcode of 00 (NOP) is forced on to the data bus. Such a harness is simple to construct and forms an extremely useful item of test equipment for performing free-run tests on the system kernel.

It is frequently beneficial to a maintenance engineer, who is likely to work on computer systems based on different types of microprocessor, to construct a similar harness for each device. Table 2.1 gives the opcodes for a no-operation instruction that can be wired into a harness for each of the main 8-bit microprocessors. The reader may like to extend this table for any particular 16-bit microprocessor that he is likely to encounter in fault-finding procedures.

Table 2.1 NOP instructions for 8-bit and 16-bit microprocessors

CPU		Data bus line								Opcode
		D7	D6	D5	D4	D3	D2	D1	D0	
Z80	Pin number:	13	10	9	7	8	12	15	14	
	NOP bit pattern:	0	0	0	0	0	0	0	0	00
8085	Pin number:	19	18	17	16	15	14	13	12	
	NOP bit pattern:	0	0	0	0	0	0	0	0	00
6502	Pin number:	26	27	28	29	30	31	32	33	
	NOP bit pattern:	1	1	1	0	1	0	1	0	EA
6809	Pin number:	24	25	26	27	28	29	30	31	
	NOP bit pattern:	0	0	0	0	0	0	0	1	01
8088/ 8086	Pin number:	9	10	11	12	13	14	15	16	
	NOP bit pattern:	1	0	0	1	0	0	0	0	90
68000	Pin number:	62	63	64	1	2	3	4	5	(D7 to D0)
	NOP bit pattern:	0	1	1	1	0	0	0	1	
	Pin number:	54	55	56	57	58	59	60	61	(D15 to D8)
	NOP bit pattern:	0	1	0	0	1	1	1	0	4E,71
Z8001	Pin number:	45	44	41	43	40	39	38	1	(D7 to D0)
	NOP bit pattern:	0	0	0	0	0	1	1	1	
	Pin number:	9	10	6	5	4	3	2	48	(D15 to D8)
	NOP bit pattern:	1	0	0	0	1	1	0	1	8D,07

(Notice that a bit setting of 0 is obtained by simply wiring to 0 V. A bit setting of 1 is obtained by wiring through a 1K resistor to +5 V. The last two microprocessors in the table – the 68000 and the Z8001 – possess 16-bit opcodes.)

If the CRO produces no activity on an address bus line during a free-run test, then it is probable that the address line is permanently shorted to +5 V or 0 V. If the same waveform is observed on two adjacent address lines, then it is probable that a short-circuit exists between them. This could be caused by a fault on the printed circuit board copper tracks but is more probably caused by a fault within one of the ICs that connect to the address bus. In this case each IC should be removed in turn, until the correct waveform is observed and the faulty IC identified. If there is no activity on any address bus lines, then the CPU itself may be faulty, or one of the faults described in section 2.3 may be the cause.

The memory address decoding circuit can also be checked using a CRO with a free-run test. Each Chip Select signal should be set in turn for each memory device while the CPU runs through the full memory map.

2.5   Static stimulus testing

The tests described so far should help to locate the cause of many catastrophic computer faults that render the machine totally unresponsive. However other fault locations in more peripheral areas of the overall computer circuit can cause the computer to fail to run its main program correctly, or to communicate correctly with the operator or other equipment.

In these cases, another item of test equipment that can be built by the test engineer is available. This equipment is a circuit board of switches and indicator LEDs that takes over the function of the CPU in the board under test. It is termed a 'Static Stimulus Tester' (SST), and can be used to examine the contents of memory and input/output devices, and even transfer data to these devices.

The method of connection of an SST to a microcomputer under test is illustrated in figure 2.9. The CPU is removed from the computer board, and a 40-pin (for an 8-bit microprocessor) plug, which terminates a ribbon cable from the SST, is placed into the vacant CPU socket. The test engineer can then 'inject' signals, by the setting of switches on the SST, into the address bus and data bus signal lines of the faulty microcomputer circuit. In this way he can examine and exercise ROM, RAM and the complete range of input/output chips that connect to the CPU.

Figure 2.10 shows the full circuit schematic for a Static Stimulus Tester for a Z80 microprocessor (figure 2.11 shows the full contact debounce circuit that must be used for each toggle switch to remove the effects of mechanical contact bounce). When the plug on the right-hand side of the diagram is plugged into the CPU socket of the board under test, access is then gained to the CPU buses of that board. The test engineer may decide

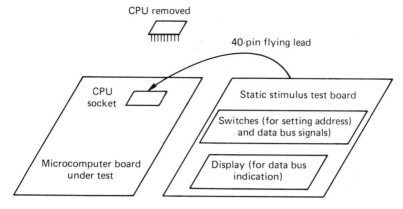

Figure 2.9 Static stimulus tester – connection to system under test

that it is sensible to examine the first few locations of the monitor ROM, and the procedure that he adopts is as follows:

(a) set the memory address of the first location in the monitor ROM on the 16 address switches;
(b) set the MREQ switch;
(c) set the RD switch.

The monitor ROM is selected through the address decoding circuit, and the contents of the first location are placed on to the data bus. The tristate buffers in the middle of the SST circuit are disabled so that the data bus switches do not connect through into the board under test. Instead, the data bits present on the data bus pass through the inverters at the bottom of the SST schematic and give indication of their status on the LEDs. This process can be repeated for any valid memory address.

A RAM location can be tested by firstly entering a test bit pattern, as follows:

(a) set the required bit pattern on the data switches;
(b) set the memory address of the chosen RAM location on the 16 address switches;
(c) set the MREQ switch;
(d) set the WR switch.

Successful writing of this data byte can then be confirmed by simply setting the RD switch in place of the WR switch and checking the LED pattern achieved against the settings of the data switches.

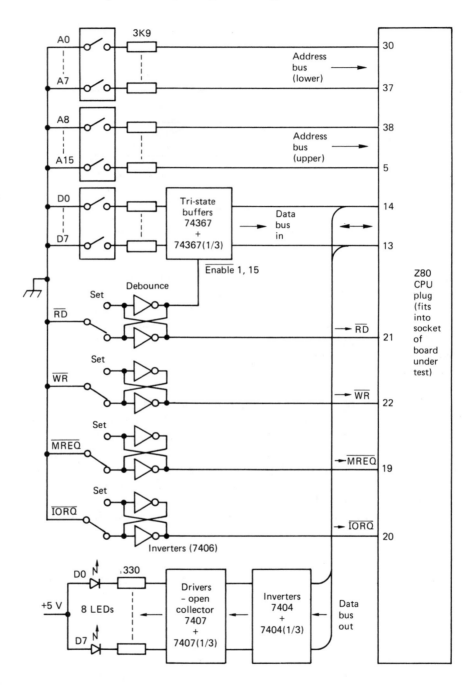

*Figure 2.10 Static stimulus tester for Z80 (see figure 2.11 for full contact
debounce circuit)*

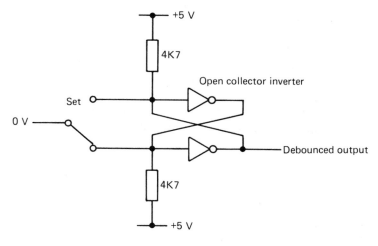

Figure 2.11 Full debounce circuit for each switch in figure 2.10

Exactly the same procedures can be adopted to check the transfer of data bytes through input/output devices, for example PIO, UART, CTC and FDC, in the circuit under test. In this case the IORQ switching must be set in place of the MREQ switch.

Although SST boards of this type are not generally commercially available, it is sensible for a test engineer who is involved in fault-finding at component level to build himself such a useful test facility. A different SST board is required for each type of microprocessor because pin numbers are not compatible between microprocessors, of course, and because different control bus signals (for example RD, WR, etc.) are used. Table 2.2 shows the different control bus lines that must be simulated by toggle switches for different microprocessors.

Table 2.2   SST control bits for different microprocessors

Microprocessor	Control bits			
Z80	RD	WR	MREQ	IORQ
8085	RD	WR	IO/M	ALE
6502	R/W			
6800	R/W	VMA		
8086	RD	WR	M/IO	ALE
68000	R/W	VMA		
Z8001	R/W	AS	B/W	N/S

Naturally the test engineer requires to understand clearly the operation of the circuit he is testing and the role of the control signals above.

An interesting variation of a Static Stimulus Tester is shown in principle in figure 2.12. In this case the flying lead from the SST board does not plug into the CPU socket of the computer under test. Instead the lead terminates in a clamp which is placed over the CPU. The SST suspends operation of the CPU by demanding DMA (Direct Memory Access) from it by the setting of the DMA Request toggle switch, and the CPU responds

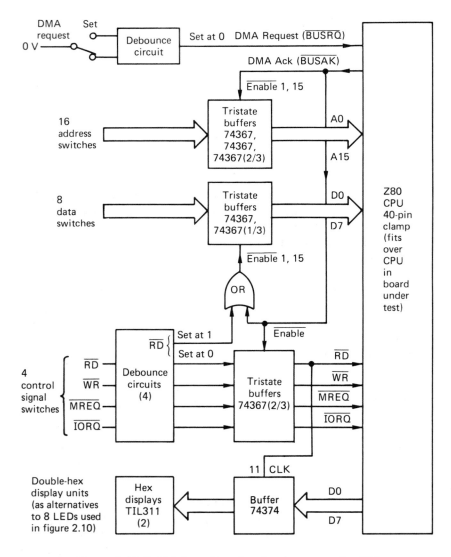

Figure 2.12 DMA-based static stimulus tester for Z80

by floating its buses and by setting the DMA Acknowledge signal. The SST then assumes control over the computer circuit, and the normal SST tests (transfer data in and out of memory and input/output devices) can then be made. The advantage of this approach is that the CPU does not have to be removed from the computer under test, but the disadvantage is that the SST circuit is somewhat more complex.

2.6 Debug EPROM

Some maintenance technicians may not have access to circuit board fabrication equipment and may not be able to construct a Static Stimulus Test board. However they may have access to an EPROM programmer. In this case an extremely useful test facility to perform some basic tests on a dead computer is an EPROM containing one or more simple test pro-grams. The computer will contain its start-up program, for example a monitor program or a bootstrap loader program, in ROM, and the debug EPROM can be used to replace this device – the monitor ROM is simply removed from its socket and the debug-EPROM is inserted in its place. Therefore when the machine is switched on, or the RESET pushbutton is pressed, the debug program will automatically be entered. The start addresses in memory of these start-up programs (that is the RESET addresses) are:

(a) Z80 – 0000
(b) 8085 – 0000
(c) 6800 – CPU examines FFFE and FFFF to find the start address
(d) 6502 – CPU examines FFFC and FFFD to find the start address
(e) 8088/ – 0000 (PC) and FFFF (Code Segment Register);
      8086 – therefore CPU starts at FFFFO (normally contains a JMP instruction)
(f) 68000 – CPU examines 000004 (4 bytes) to find the start address (and loads contents of 000000 into Supervisor Stack Pointer)
(g) Z8001 – 0006 (16-bit offset) and 0004 (PC segment number). Contents of 0000 are loaded into Flags.

The test engineer has to decide what type of test programs should be placed in the debug-EPROM. It may be sensible to prepare several EPROMs, each with its own single test program that exercises different parts of the system, for example memory or input/output. Useful test programs (using Z80 mnemonics) are as follows.

Test program A – 'loop stop'

```
HERE : JP HERE        ; Jump to instruction labelled HERE
```

This single-instruction program, which is 3-bytes long for an 8-bit microprocessor, repetitively obeys the same instruction. Its value is that a CRO will trigger on the short cycle of repetitive activity, and the three following stages in the fetch–execute cycle can be monitored on the data bus and address bus:

(a) fetch – read the opcode from memory for example address 0000;
(b) execute 1 – read the second byte of the instruction from memory (this is the least-significant half of the memory address of the instruction);
(c) execute 2 – read the third byte of the instruction from memory (this is the most-significant half of the memory address of the instruction).

In this way the fetch–execute cycle of the CPU can be checked – this is a similar test, but not as exhaustive, as the NOP test described earlier in this chapter. It confirms correct operation of the system kernel. If the bit pattern observed on any chosen data bus line, for example D7 (which should show the state of the most-significant bit in each byte), for the three stages in the execution of this instruction is incorrect, then the CRO could be used to check the state of any control bus lines which could inhibit CPU operation. Additionally the CS (Chip Select) line to the debug-EPROM could be checked for activity.

Test program B – input/output check

```
START: IN A, (40H)    ;Input from I/O (port) address 40
       OUT (41H), A ;Output to I/O (port) address 41
       LD (3000H), A ;Store in memory at location 3000
       JP START       ;Repeat
```

Signals on the input port can be set, perhaps simply by using a length of wire to connect logic 1 (+5 V) or 0 (0 V) to a port line. This bit setting should then be observed on the corresponding output port line, for example using a CRO. Additionally the control bus lines used for memory and input/output transfers can be checked.

Test program C – terminal check

```
POLL: IN A, (61H)    ;Input UART status register
      AND 1          ;Check bit 1
      JP Z,POLL      ;Jump if bit 1 is 0 (UART is busy)
```

```
LD A,58H      ;Load A with ASCII for letter X
OUT (60H),A   ;Output to UART Tx (transmit)
JP POLL       ;Repeat
```

This program continually outputs the character X to the serial-driven terminal on the computer. This confirms correct CPU operation, debug-EPROM addressing, input/output handling and terminal (VDU) operation. If the CRT display device is driven directly from computer memory, and not by RS232-C serial link, then the test program should simply store a chosen character in consecutive locations in the video RAM area for the machine.

Test program D – memory check

More rigorous memory test programs, particularly for RAM, can be built into the debug-EPROM. Such test programs are described in detail in Chapter 4. It is possible to include several such test programs into a single debug-EPROM, which is entered on RESET (or machine switch-on). The choice of which test program is to be run could be determined by the setting of some convenient switches on an input port. If no such switch facility exists on the machine under test, then a length of wire could be used to simulate a switch setting on an input port. If there is no input port available, then it may be beneficial to build an input port, with switches, on a separate test board that is connected in some way to the computer board under test. The additional input port (simply a TTL buffer requiring only data bus connections and a simple address decoding circuit) must fit into a blank position in the input/output map for the system under test.

2.7 Miscellaneous factors

There are many environmental factors that affect the performance of electronic systems and computers. Additionally the maintenance technician or test engineer soon develops a familiarity with certain fault types and their causes. It is worth emphasising a point made at the beginning of this chapter about the nature of faults in computer systems. Most faults are electro-mechanical in nature and are not caused by failure of complex ICs – the author has never experienced the failure of a microprocessor for example. The following list of fault categories is presented in order of frequency of occurrence:

(a) Electro-mechanical faults – floppy disk not loaded properly, floppy disk drive failure (drive belt, stepper motor, dirty head, etc.), pushbutton failure, plug/socket connection fault.

(b) Power supply failure – either ac mains or dc power supply unit (fuse, regulator, smoothing capacitor, etc.); even a temporary loss of supply can 'scramble' a computer's RAM.
(c) Open-circuit – dry joint (broken solder connection), loose IC pin in socket, broken component wire (particularly if component stands proud of circuit board), wire connection failure (soldered, crimped or screwed), edge connector, crack in copper track.
(d) Short-circuit – touching components wires, bridge across copper tracks, moisture.
(e) Faulty component – IC or discrete component.
(f) Others – overheating, interference.

Notice that most of these fault types can either be detected visually or with a minimum of test equipment. If test equipment is required, firstly ensure that it is working correctly – it may be necessary to calibrate it, for example a CRO or DVM.

Never trust a non-technical operator fully. He may report a fault, whereas he is simply not performing the correct procedure to start the computer or is not entering the correct command to call the required program/package. He may have just disconnected the cable connection to one of the computer's peripherals, or he may have inadvertently performed a 'drop test' on the machine. Find out the recent history of the system before the fault became apparent.

Some faults are heat-dependent. If a computer works correctly for some time after switch-on, but then subsequently fails, it is probable that some part of the system is overheating. Normally this is due to a component, for example an IC, that operates marginally when cool, although the fault could be related to metallic expansion of conductors, etc. It may be found that operating the system with the case or housing removed produces a longer period of correct operation. The failure of a cooling fan, or the uneven distribution of cooling air flow due to a blockage, may be the cause of the overheating. Whatever the cause, a very simple procedure (not requiring any test equipment) may help to locate the fault. The application of a cooling spray to different components in turn around the board/boards often chills the overheated area to produce instantaneous correct operation. In a similar way an overheating fault can be deliberately aggravated by the operator in order to induce the fault faster by means of a heat gun – this is similar to a small electric hair-dryer. These techniques help to identify the precise component that is faulty.

Occasionally the deposition of moisture from the atmosphere can cause short-circuits around a board. This problem may show itself by the failure of the computer to operate when first switched on, but after some time the heating effect of the circuit components may drive off the moisture and the system will become operational.

Some severely overheated and perhaps irretrievably damaged components can be detected visually, for example an IC that is discoloured from black to grey, a cracked IC or a domed IC.

There is a fundamental difference between servicing mechanical equipment and servicing electronic equipment. While much mechanical equipment requires regular adjustment, replacement, lubrication, etc., the maxim that should be followed for much electronic equipment is 'if it works, leave it alone'. Casual board replacement, component removal, etc., is quite likely to introduce faults. However when boards have to be removed from edge connectors or back planes, a quick visual inspection of the state of the gold tracks (which overlay the copper tracks in order to carry signals off the board) on the edge of the board may show dirt and oxidation deposits. This deposition may cause open-circuits and should be cleaned off with a pencil eraser. Application of a cleaning spray may help to remove dirt in edge connectors.

A final piece of advice may make the task of monitoring IC interconnection pins with a variety of test equipment easier. To prevent the test probe possibly shorting across adjacent pins, the placing of a IC clip over the IC under test and then connection of the equipment probe to the connectors at the top of the clip should facilitate easier connection.

Bibliography

1. Robert T. Paynter, *Microcomputer Operation, Troubleshooting and Repair,* Prentice-Hall, 1986.

3 Board Testing

3.1 Logic probe, logic pulser and current tracer

A range of simple hand-held test equipment is available for monitoring logic levels in systems under test. The first group of three devices in this range (logic probe, logic pulser and current tracer) are useful in tracing faults in computer CPU boards that are inoperative, and these devices are described next. Further devices are described in the following sections.

Figure 3.1 shows the combined use of a logic probe and logic pulser for testing a simple OR gate. Both devices derive dc power from the circuit board under test, that is the +5 V and 0 V clips must be placed across the dc power rails. Operation of the pushbutton on the logic pulser injects pulses into the circuit node – the input to the OR gate in this case. The indicator LEDs on the logic probe should respond to these stimuli. Typically the logic probe indicator LEDs are: red (for logic 1), green (for logic 0) and amber (for floating, or unconnected, signal level). The use of the two instruments can be extended to locate interconnection faults around a circuit board, for example along a copper track to highlight an open-circuit crack or a short-circuit between tracks. Additionally the logic probe can be used on its own to indicate fixed logic levels, or pulse activity (the LEDs blink, as described in the following paragraphs). Activity on

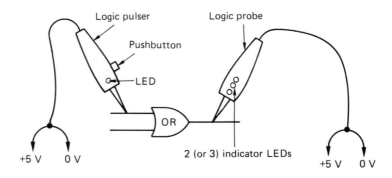

Figure 3.1 Use of logic probe and logic pulser

computer address and data bus links can be confirmed to indicate that the system kernel is active.

Logic probes vary from simple devices, with only two indicator LEDs (one lit for logic 1, other lit for logic 0, both lit dimly for floating signal), to devices that include 'pulse stretching' (to slow down the pulse rate to flash the LEDs at a speed that can be detected visually). Figure 3.2 shows the circuit diagram for two types of logic probe. In (a), two Schmitt trigger circuits are employed to ensure that only one indicator LED is lit; while in (b), a third (amber) LED lights when the probe signal is between the two voltage trigger levels. These levels are normally

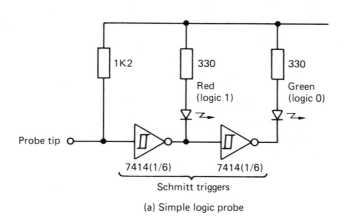

(a) Simple logic probe

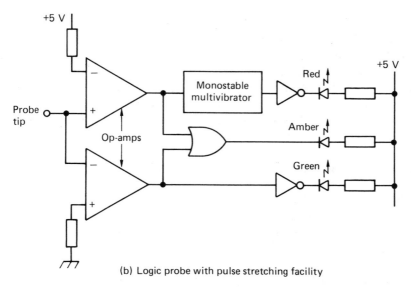

(b) Logic probe with pulse stretching facility

Figure 3.2 Logic probe circuits

logic 1 – above 2 V
logic 0 – below 0.8 V

for TTL circuits. The use of a monostable multivibrator in (b) slows the flash rate of the red indicator LED to a speed of typically 10 Hz to indicate pulse activity at the test point. One disadvantage of the use of op-amps as input threshold detectors in (b) is the high-frequency limitation (typically 500 kHz) of the device. The logic probes shown in figure 3.2 are only suitable for TTL circuits. Different logic probe circuits are required for CMOS circuits, which can use between +3 V and +18 V for the positive dc supply rail voltage. In this case the threshold voltages are not 2 V and 0.8 V, but are expressed as fractions of the dc rail voltage, namely 0.7VDD and 0.3VDD (VDD = rail voltage). Some proprietary logic probes offer a switch facility to select either TTL or CMOS operation. Protection against over-voltage and polarity reversal is normally provided, and some logic probes will detect pulses as narrow as 10 nanoseconds.

Logic pulsers produce high current pulses of short duration, such that they will over-ride signal levels existing at the circuit node to which they are connected without causing damage. Typically the pressing of a pushbutton, together with the setting of a mode switch on the device, will inject one of the following:

(a) single pulse;
(b) burst of pulses, for example 10 or 100 pulses;
(c) continuous pulses.

When the pushbutton is not pressed, the pulser tip is at the floating (high impedance) level. Several logic pulsers check the existing logic level of the circuit node before a pulse is injected, so that the logic level is inverted in the formation of the injected pulse.

The combined use of a logic probe and logic pulser is an effective way of locating many faulty ICs (particularly TTL devices) or circuit connections on computer boards. However some faults are more easily tackled using a current tracer in place of a logic probe. Figure 3.3 shows the appearance of a typical current tracer. There are two primary differences between the operation of a current tracer compared with a logic probe:

(a) the current tracer measures current, and not voltage levels;
(b) the current tracer responds only to ac (or pulse) signals – it does not respond to steady dc levels, for example +5 V and 0 V, as does the logic probe.

The inductive pick-up feature, which is based on the simple transformer principle, means that the alignment of the tracer tip is important. The

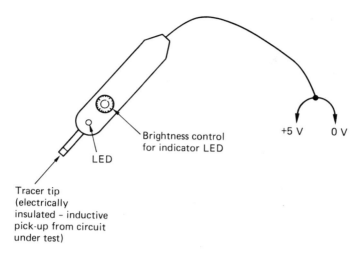

Brightness control
for indicator LED

+5 V   0 V

LED

Tracer tip
(electrically
insulated – inductive
pick-up from circuit
under test)

Figure 3.3 Current tracer

current tracer must be placed perpendicular to the copper track (or whatever other conductor is being examined), and also must be aligned in the direction of current flow. For this latter reason, an alignment spot is usually marked on the tracer tip. Additionally a potentiometer adjustment is included to allow the operator to adjust the illumination level of the indicator LED to suit his particular preference, and a pulse stretching facility is included.

Proficient skill in the use of the current tracer is not easy to acquire because the operator must be careful to align the tip correctly as he follows a conduction path around a circuit, for example through right-angle and T-connections on copper track systems. Additionally, care must be taken not to overlap two adjacent conductors, for example copper tracks, with the tracer tip. However the value of a current tracer, when used in conjunction with a logic pulser, for locating certain types of faults in inactive circuit boards, is illustrated in figure 3.4. Consider the common fault in (a) that occurs when the positive dc rail voltage is low due to a short-circuit across the two rails by a faulty component. Normally the faulty component is not an IC, which frequently fails catastrophically with signs of damage to the IC, for example a 'dome' eruption on the top of the IC package due to overheating of the silicon wafer within. The fault is more likely to be caused by one of the decoupling capacitors (typically small ceramic disc capacitors) that are placed across every one or two ICs. The +5 V rail is disconnected from the power supply, which now produces the full +5 V voltage level. Pulses are injected into the positive dc rail as shown, and traced along the rail with the current tracer until they disappear (no indication on the current tracer LED). The location of the

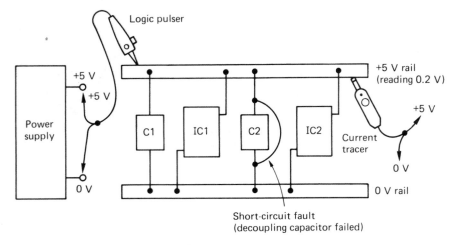

(a) Short-circuit across +5 V and 0 V dc rails

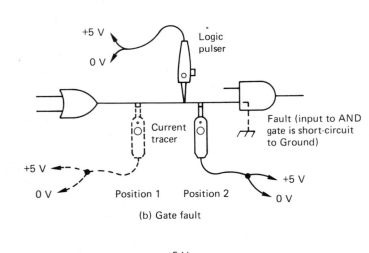

(b) Gate fault

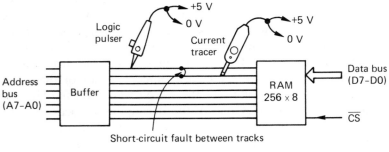

(c) Printed circuit board fault

Figure 3.4 Use of current tracer and logic pulser

fault has now been traced. The faulty decoupling capacitor should then be removed.

In figure 3.4(b) measurement by a CRO or logic probe shows that the connection between two gates is stuck at a fault level of 0 V. This could be caused by a short-circuit to Ground (0 V) at the output of the first gate, at the input to the second gate or along the printed circuit board interconnecting copper track. The fault is located by following pulses, which are injected at a midway point between the two gates, into the second gate.

A short-circuit fault between adjacent copper tracks is illustrated in figure 3.4(c). Sliding the current tracer along the copper track until pulses disappear indicates the location of the short-circuit. Such faults are often caused by solder splashes or the introduction of conducting foreign-bodies, for example wire offcuts.

3.2 Logic monitor and logic comparator

Two further items of test equipment are available for testing individual ICs. Figure 3.5 shows a logic monitor (or 'logic clip') which can be placed over an IC under test. The device draws dc power from the IC, and it is basically a multi-way logic probe (without pulse stretching). The LEDs therefore illuminate in response to the voltage levels present at the IC interconnection pins. This device is only normally of value for testing circuits with steady or infrequently changing signals, and logic monitors for 8-, 14- and 16-pin TTL ICs are available – a 16-pin logic monitor can often be used on smaller ICs. Pulse activity is indicated by a LED intensity less than the full illumination for a fixed +5 V (for example the positive dc supply pin) – the intensity is proportional to the duty cycle of the pulse stream. A more useful, but more expensive, item of test equipment is a logic comparator, which is used for testing the correct operation of an individual IC while it is active within its normal circuit configuration.

Figure 3.6 illustrates the principle of operation of a logic comparator, which possesses a flying lead that terminates in a clip. The clip is placed

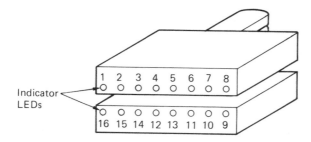

Figure 3.5 Logic monitor (or 'logic clip')

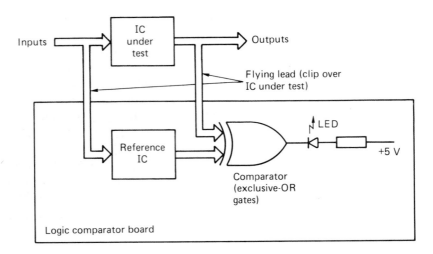

Figure 3.6 Logic comparator

over the IC under test, so that the reference IC and the test IC, which are of exactly the same type (for example NAND gates), receive identical input signals and should therefore produce identical output signals at all times. The outputs of each IC are compared using exclusive-OR gates, and if any signal differences occur – because of a faulty test IC – an indicator LED lights. Clearly a different logic comparator circuit board is needed for each different IC-type. This can prove to be expensive for many repair workshops, although it is possible to be selective and choose logic comparators for particular ICs (for example gates, inverters or buffers) that are commonly encountered in equipment that is repaired regularly. There is at least one logic comparator available that offers the flexible selection of several different types of reference IC.

3.3   Computer-based IC testers

The devices described in the previous sections can test most ICs, perhaps totally or partially, and additionally can be applied to help locate faults in the interconnections between ICs, for example copper track faults. However a range of microcomputer-based test equipment has been developed that provides far more comprehensive testing facilities. A single piece of equipment can test a large range of ICs, for example the TTL range of digital ICs, the CMOS equivalent series, plus memory and even analogue ICs. This type of equipment is a much cheaper alternative to a full ATE (Automatic Test Equipment) system, as used at the end of many production lines in electronic assembly factories. An ATE system, which is also computer-based, tests a full circuit board, and can be programmed to test different boards. Several injected stimulus signals can be specified at different circuit nodes, and response signals recorded in order to give an indication of correct or incorrect board operation.

The first of the microcomputer-based IC testers described in this section injects a low-frequency sinewave across two IC pins, and displays on a CRT the current–voltage waveform for those circuit points. Figure 3.7 shows how such a tester is connected to a SUT (System Under Test). One end of the interconnecting ribbon cable is plugged into a socket in the tester, and the other end is clamped over the IC under test – the IC under test could be removed from its circuit board and inserted into the test IC socket in the tester if preferred. The tester injects a signal (typically 50 Hz, or 2 kHz) across two selected pins and the resulting current–voltage waveform is displayed on the CRT. This waveform can be interpreted to judge correct or incorrect operation of the circuit component, for example PN junction. Alternatively a reference IC can be used and two waveforms displayed in order to highlight differences and indicate faults more clearly. This tester is suitable for testing capacitors, diodes, transistors, voltage regulators, op-amps (shown in figure 3.7), digital ICs, and others. The system under test must be unpowered, and the current-limited nature of the injected signal ensures that components under test are not damaged.

A more powerful version of the current–voltage waveform tester is illustrated in figure 3.8. In this arrangement the waveforms for all pins on

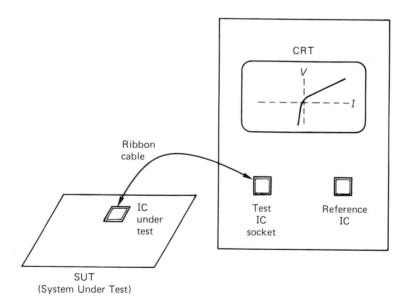

Figure 3.7 Current/voltage IC tester

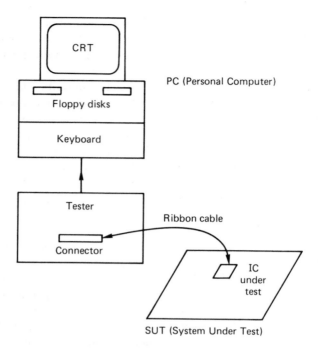

Figure 3.8 PC-based current/voltage IC tester

the IC are held on the PC floppy disk in digitised form. Firstly a good board is tested, and the test data for an IC (or all ICs if required) are stored on floppy. Later when a board is faulty, its test data are measured and compared by the PC with the reference data. Differences are highlighted to indicate faulty ICs. Software within the PC notifies the operator which flying-lead ribbon cable and which IC to test. This system provides a very simple and quick test procedure for suspect boards.

A variation of the current–voltage test procedure is one that performs a functional test on a digital IC. Such a microcomputer-based tester is shown in figure 3.9. The tester sets input signals and records output signal levels to test for correct operation; the component under test may be a counter or a buffer, for example. Logic levels for all pins on an IC are indicated on the CRT, and incorrect signals are highlighted. An IC can be tested 'in-circuit', using the interconnecting ribbon cable, or 'out-of-circuit', by placing it in a ZIF (Zero Insertion Force) socket on the front panel of the tester. Therefore a test procedure on a suspect board consists of connecting a clip over each IC in turn and requesting a test/compare operation for each device. Additionally the tester can be requested to identify a digital IC type from its library – this is particularly useful with unmarked ICs.

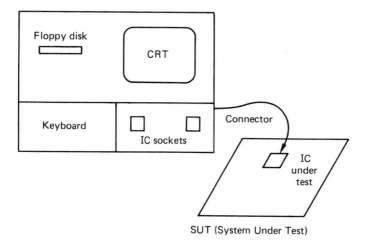

Figure 3.9 IC functional tester

Bibliography

1. G. B. Williams, *Troubleshooting on Microprocessor Based Systems,* Pergamon, 1984.

4   Diagnostic Software

4.1   Introduction

One of the best ways of testing parts of an overall hardware configuration is to use the flexibility and intelligence of the CPU in running various test programs that exercise the hardware in different ways. In an ideal world such software tests would be performed automatically by a computer when it is switched on (or reset). Unfortunately few system designers build such routines into the start-up program (for example a ROM-based bootstrap loader), or alternatively only a simple memory test is performed. Consequently the maintenance engineer is required to produce his own test programs, perhaps with supporting additional hardware, to perform these tests.

The nature of software diagnostics requires that at least the system kernel is operational, as can be verified by a NOP test described earlier. The following methods of implementing software diagnostics are available:

(a) Automatic tests performed when the computer is switched on, and normally held in the ROM that contains the start-up program. Typically such a test routine produces a message on the CRT display, for example 'SYSTEM OK' or '512K RAM MEMORY OK', after successfully performing a sequence of writing to and reading from every RAM memory location.
(b) A 'monitor ROM' (typically in EPROM) that is additional to the start-up ROM, and contains a range of hardware test routines. This device fits permanently into the memory map of the computer, and the particular test required is specified by the operator using the system keyboard.
(c) The software diagnostics must be loaded into the machine by the maintenance engineer. Typically this involves transferring the programs from hard disk, floppy disk or cassette recorder, or alternatively replacing an existing ROM/EPROM with a similar device containing the test program/programs. It is also possible manually to enter a test program written either in assembly language or even in BASIC into RAM and then execute the program.

These procedures are described in the following sections.

4.2 Start-up ROM

While the simplest boot program held in ROM may not contain any automatic test routines, it can be regarded as indicating correct hardware operation if the operating system prompt (for example C>) appears on the CRT. A successful boot operation confirms correct operation of:

(a) power supplies;
(b) system kernel;
(c) ROM containing start-up program;
(d) some RAM (for example area used for stack by bootstrap loader program);
(e) backing store (whichever of hard disk or floppy disk that system boots off);
(f) CRT drive (either RS232-C link to VDU, or video generation circuit from system RAM).

This is a significant proportion of most computer hardware configurations. Clearly failure to boot successfully could be caused by a fault in any of these areas.

Some start-up programs perform a limited range of additional test routines. The most common is a memory test. RAM is tested by a write/read cycle for each location. An error message is displayed if a memory location fails the test, or an alternative message confirms correct operation of the complete block of system RAM. Additionally this test program can be used to locate the end of system RAM, or the end of functional RAM, by noting that the first address at which the write/read test fails is on a memory boundary, for example after 256K. The results of this test are used for two purposes:

(1) to indicate the available memory space to the operator, for example a '256K RAM MEMORY' message is produced on the CRT;
(2) to indicate to the operating system the working RAM capacity – a larger RAM memory space could cause the bootstrap loader to load the operating system into a different part of RAM; additionally larger files can be transferred from backing store without segmention.

The start-up program could also perform simple ROM checks, for example a 'checksum' test, as described in section 4.4.

4.3 Monitor ROM

Some computer configurations include a ROM-based 'monitor' program that allows the operator to enter and test machine code programs and to test parts of the hardware. Entry into the monitor program may be by one of a variety of procedures, for example setting a link on the CPU board and resetting the machine, pressing a pushbutton that generates an interrupt, or implementing a specific command to the operating system.

Two different types of monitor program, that perform hardware testing, are presented in this section. Table 4.1 lists examples of the commands available to the operator in a monitor ROM placed in an 8-bit microcomputer system.

Table 4.1   Typical monitor ROM operator commands – version A
(*Note:* the monitor prompt on the CRT is ".")

Command	Action
.E 0A72	Displays contents of memory location OA72 (hex) and allows the user to alter the contents by entering two hex digits
.D 3000 3100	Displays contents of memory locations 3000 (hex) to 3100
.T 8000 FFFF	Tests RAM (writing/reading 1s and 0s for every location) between addresses 8000 and FFFF – displays 'P' for pass, or alternatively a failure message
.X	Displays the contents of the CPU registers
.0 80 55	Outputs the byte 55 (hex) to input/output address 80 (hex)
.I 81	Input, and display, from input/output address 81 (hex)
.W 2000 1 12 03 2	Write 2 sectors from memory, starting at location 2000, to disk drive 1, commencing at track 12 and sector 03
.R 3000 0 49 09 1	Read 1 sector to memory, starting at location 3000, from disk drive 0, commencing at track 49 and sector 09
.G 0500	Go to memory location 0500, that is enter the program starting at this address
.B 120E	Set a breakpoint at memory location 120E (must be in RAM) – program execution is suspended at that point and the monitor program is re-entered

Examination of these facilities shows that:

(a) ROM locations can be examined;
(b) RAM can be tested (using a write/read cycle);
(c) input/output devices can be tested – data can be transferred in and out through PIOs, non-programmable ports, UARTs, CTCs, FDCs, etc.)
(d) Test programs can be entered into RAM in machine code and then executed.

An alternative form of monitor program that allows the operator to call different test functions produces the typical screen display shown:

Menu display for monitor ROM – version B

```
    Hardware Diagnostic

Please enter a number to select system to be tested.

    1 – ROM
    2 – RAM
    3 – CRT display
    4 – Keyboard
    5 – Floppy
    6 – Parallel printer
    7 – Serial link

Alternatively press SPACE to return to operating system.
```

In this version, the operator commands are at a 'higher level', that is a simple numerical entry initiates a full test of part of the hardware configuration. In the previous version, the operator must have a detailed understanding of the hardware system, including knowledge of the memory map and input/output map.

4.4 Entered test programs

In this section, test programs that must be entered manually, or transferred from disk or cassette recorder, are described. Additionally the test programs could reside in EPROMs that can be placed in the sockets for either the start-up (bootstrap) ROM or the monitor ROM – figure 4.1 shows the arrangement. This latter method is to be preferred because faults in the input/output hardware can prevent successful loading of the

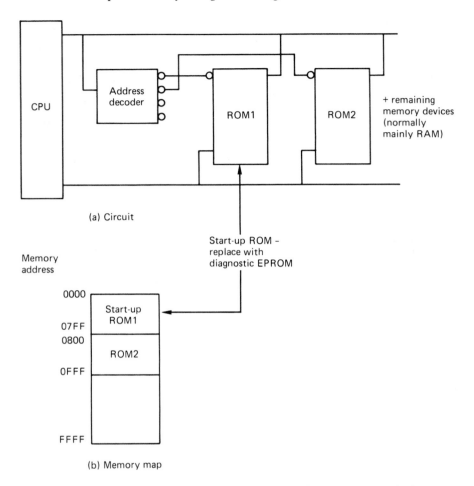

(a) Circuit

(b) Memory map

Figure 4.1 Repalcing start-up ROM with diagnostic EPROM

test programs from peripheral devices. Whatever the source of the test programs, the diagnostic operations they perform are similar to those described in the previous two sections. Typical test programs are described next.

(a) ROM checksum test

Confirming that the contents of any ROM device are correct would appear to be a difficult task for a test program to perform unless an identically programmed ROM is available for comparison purposes. However many ROM/PROM/EPROM devices store a 'checksum' in the last location. The checksum is the sum of the contents of all previous memory locations, excluding carry bits, in the device. The task therefore for a ROM diagnostic program is to add the contents of all locations, excluding the last loction, and to compare the sum with the contents of the last location. A flowchart for such a program is shown in figure 4.2. A program listing for a Z80-based system then follows.

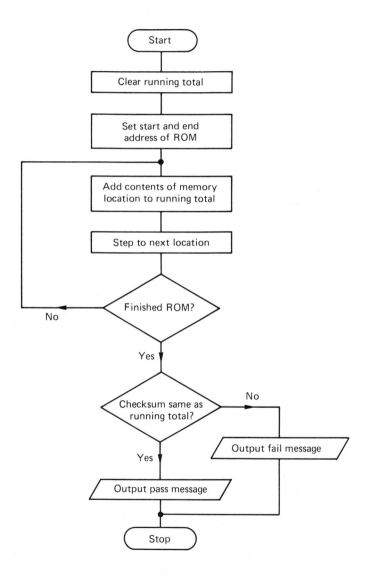

Figure 4.2 Flowchart of ROM checksum test program

Program listing for ROM Checksum test program

```
            ORG   0000H          ;Test program start address of 0000
ROMFIRST EQU   3000H             ;Address range
  ROMLAST EQU   33FFH            ;               of ROM under test
            LD    A,0            ;Clear A
            LD    E,0            ;       and E
            LD    BC,ROMFIRST    ;Set first address of ROM in BC
            LD    HL,ROMLAST     ;Set last address of ROM in HL
   REPEAT: DEC   HL              ;Step back 1 location from ROMLAST
            LD    A,(HL)         ;Read byte from memory
            ADD   A,E            ;Add to running total
            LD    E,A            ;Store in E
            XOR   A              ;Clear carry flag
            PUSH  HL             ;Preserve HL on stack
            SBC   HL,BC          ;Subtract ROMFIRST from current addr.
            POP   HL             ;Reinstate HL from stack
            JP    NZ,REPEAT      ;Repeat if not finished ROM
            LD    HL,ROMLAST     ;Address of checksum
            CP    (HL)           ;Compare checksum with running total
            JP    NZ,FAILURE     ;Jump if different
SUCCESS: CALL  PASSMESS          ;Display pass message
            HALT
FAILURE: CALL  FAILMESS          ;Display fail message
            HALT
```

The EQU (equate) statements need to be altered to suit the address range of the ROM in the circuit under test. Additionally, subroutines PASS-MESS and FAILMESS need to be written to display the result of the test to the operator; alternatively some other indication may be given to the operator, for example the lighting of a LED or the sounding of a buzzer/loudspeaker.

(b) RAM check

Write/read cycles must be successfully completed for each memory location within the RAM memory space. There are many ways in which this can be performed, for example:

(1) zero test (write binary 0000 0000 into each location, and confirm successful transfer by reading the byte back from the RAM location) – the first half of this test is often performed on the video-RAM area within a computer when the machine is switched on in order to clear the CRT display;

(2) 'chequerboard' test (write 1010 1010, AA in hex, and then 0101 0101, 55 in hex, into each location, followed by a read-back check);

(3) 'walking one's' test (0000 0000, then 0000 0001, then 0000 0010, then 0000 0100, etc.);

(4) binary count test (hex 00, then 01, then 02, then 03, etc.).

The flowchart for a zero test is shown in figure 4.3. The program listing for a Z80-based chequerboard test program then follows.

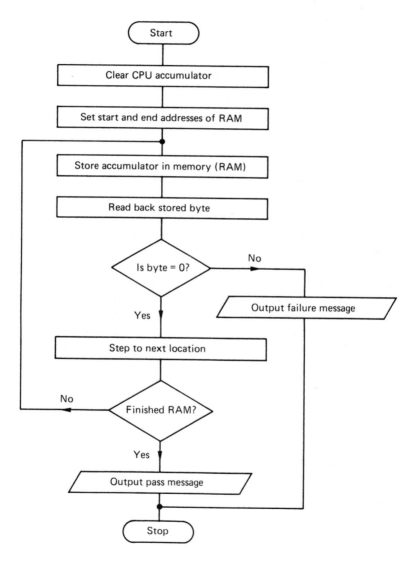

Figure 4.3 Flowchart of RAM zero test progam

Program listing for RAM chequerboard test program

```
            ORG    0000H        ;Test program start address of 0000
RAMFIRST EQU    0800H        ;Address range
RAMLAST  EQU    0FFFH        ;              of RAM under test
   START: LD     BC,RAMFIRST  ;Set first address of RAM in BC
  REPEAT: LD     HL,RAMLAST   ;Set last address of RAM in HL
           LD     A,0AAH       ;Bit pattern of 1010 1010
           LD     (BC),A       ;Store into memory
           LD     A,(BC)       ;Retrieve from memory
           CP     0AAH         ;Compare with original value
           CALL   NZ,FAILMESS  ;Display failure message if different
           LD     A,55H        ;Bit pattern of 0101 0101
           LD     (BC),A       ;Store into memory
           LD     A,(BC)       ;Retrieve from memory
           CP     55H          ;Compare with original value
           CALL   NZ,FAILMESS  ;Display failure message if different
           INC    BC           ;Step to next location
           XOR    A            ;Clear carry flag
           SBC    HL,BC        ;Subtract current address from RAMLAST
           JP     NZ,REPEAT    ;Repeat if not finished RAM
           CALL   PASSMESS     ;Display P (for Pass)
           JP     START        ;Repeat the entire test
```

Notice that the convention of RAM test programs is to display the letter P (for Pass) after each complete test of the required RAM area. A typical test procedure is to 'soak-test' the RAM, that is allow the program to cycle repetitively for some time.

An alternative way of checking RAM is to enter and run a high-level language program that tests a block of RAM locations. Most home and office computers possess a BASIC interpreter, and in most BASIC implementations the POKE (write a data byte into a location) and PEEK (read a data byte from a location) instructions are available. The following BASIC program performs the same type of chequerboard test function as the assembly language program just described.

Program listing for RAM chequerboard test program (in BASIC)

```
10 REM RAM TEST PROGRAM
20 REM SET RAM START ADDRESS
30 LET START=0
40 REM SET RAM END ADDRESS
50 LET END=32767
60 LET FIRST%=85
70 LET SECOND%=170
80 FOR I=START TO END
90 REM PRESERVE RAM CONTENTS
100 STORE%=PEEK(I)
110 REM NOW TEST LOCATION
```

```
120 POKE I,FIRST%
130 Y%=PEEK(I)
140 IF Y%<>FIRST% GOTO 230
150 POKE I,SECOND%
160 Z%=PEEK(I)
170 IF Z%<>SECOND% GOTO 230
180 REM REINSTATE RAM CONTENTS
190 POKE I,STORE%
200 NEXT I
210 PRINT "SUCCESSFUL RAM TEST"
220 GOTO 80
230 PRINT "FAILURE AT LOCATION",I
240 GOTO 190
```

Notice that this program recognises that a RAM test overwrites the contents of memory locations, including the area in which the test program itself resides. Hence the contents of each memory location are preserved before each location is tested, and reinstated after the test.

(c) Input/output port test

Input/output ports are either part of a PIO (Programmable Input/Output) or form separate TTL devices, for example SN74LS244 (input port) and SN74LS373 (output port). They are used to connect the computer to external devices, for example parallel printers, segment displays, LED indicators and pushbuttons. Diagnostic software can either test ports with these external devices connected, or the connections (typically plug/socket) can be broken before testing takes place. Figure 4.4 shows a typical input/output port configuration (a PIO in this case). The following tests can be made.

Test A (output port only)

Simply output a test byte, and confirm correct bit setting with a CRO or DVM, for example for a Z80 system:

```
LD   A,55H      ;Set A to 0101 0101
OUT  (PORTADDR),A ;Output to I/O address PORTADDR
```

An alternative test program that outputs a binary count on the 8 port lines is

```
      LD   A,0
LOOP: OUT  (PORTADDR),A
      INC  A
      JP   LOOP
```

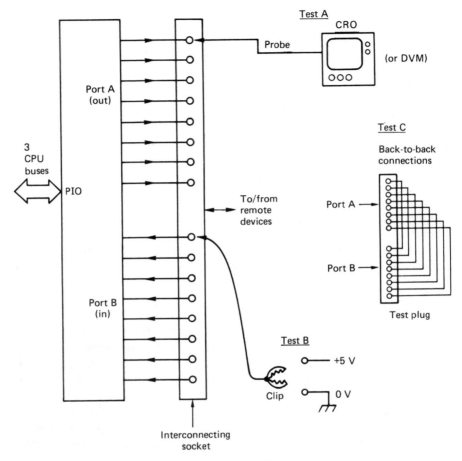

Figure 4.4 Tesy arrangements for input/output ports

Different frequency pulse waveforms will be observed with a CRO on each port line.

Test B

Connect a flying lead between an input port line and either +5 V or 0 V, and test the setting of the input port as follows:

```
LOOP: IN    A, (INPORT)
      OUT   (OUTPORT) , A
      JP    LOOP
```

The program loops continuously, and the setting of each input port line can be examined with a CRO or DVM on the corresponding bit on the output port. This test confirms correct operation of both input and output ports.

Test C

A test plug can be prepared with each output port line connected back in to the corresponding input port line. The following test program (written in Z80 assembly language) exercises both output and input ports:

```
START: LD   A, 00
       OUT  (OUTPORT) , A   ; Output 00 to output port
       IN   A, (INPORT)     ; Read back in through input
                              port
       CP   00H             ; Same?
       JP   NZ, FAILURE     ; If not, indicate the failure
       LD   A, 0FFH
       OUT  (OUTPORT) , A   ; Output FF to output port
       IN   A, (INPORT)     ; Read back in through input
                              port
       CP   0FFH            ; Same?
       JP   NZ, FAILURE     ; If not, indicate the failure
       JP   START           ; Repeat program
```

If the ports are operating correctly, a pulse waveform will be observed on a CRO on the back-to-back connections.

In the case of each of the above test programs, it has been assumed that if the ports form part of a PIO then the PIO has been correctly initialised (that is port directions selected). If this is not the case, each program must be preceded with

```
       LD   A,CONTBYTE    ;Set control byte into A
       OUT  (PIOCONT),A   ;Output to control register in PIO
```

It is possible to duplicate these assembly language (entered into memory in machine code of course) test programs in BASIC. However the computer system under test must use memory mapped input/output (input/output devices are treated as if they are memory devices), so that the PEEK and POKE instructions can be used to transfer bytes through input/output ports. The BASIC equivalent of the program for Test C above is

```
10 REM INPUT/OUTPUT PORT TEST PROGRAM
20 REM SET ADDRESS OF OUTPUT PORT
30 LET OUTPUT=65120
```

```
40 REM SET ADDRESS OF INPUT PORT
50 LET INPORT=65121
60 LET FIRST%=0
70 POKE OUTPUT,FIRST%
80 BACK%=PEEK (INPORT)
90 IF BACK%<>FIRST% GOTO 160
100 LET SECOND%=255
110 POKE OUTPORT,SECOND%
120 BACK%=PEEK (INPORT)
130 IF BACK%<>SECOND% GOTO 160
140 PRINT "SUCCESSFUL TEST"
150 GOTO 10
160 PRINT "I/O PORT FAILURE"
```

Some BASIC implementations possess the OUT and INP commands, and in these cases input/output ports can be tested if the I/O system is not memory mapped.

More specialised input/output testing, for example floppy disk, parallel printer and serial VDU, is described in the next chapter.

Bibliography

1. G. B. Williams, *Troubleshooting on Microprocessor Systems,* Pergamon, 1984.
2. M. Tooley, *Servicing Personal Computers,* Newnes, 1985.

5 Peripheral Testing

5.1 Introduction

Computer peripherals include VDUs (terminals), printers, backing stores (floppy disks and hard disks) and magnetic tape devices (digital cassettes and audio cassettes). The electro-mechanical nature, with the inherent associated unreliability, of much of this type of equipment means that frequently the cause of an overall system fault is the breakdown of a peripheral. Sometimes the computer system is still operative, but is downgraded, for example when a printer fails. Testing techniques and the natures of peripheral faults are described in this chapter.

5.2 VDUS and serial devices

VDUs (or 'terminals') are serial-drive devices that are connected to computers via the world-standard RS232-C interface (or 'V24 interface'). A VDU possesses a CRT and keyboard, and performs the role of an interactive operator terminal to the computer. Serial data interfaces are also applied from computers to graph plotters, EPROM programmers, other computers and to serial-drive printers (although most printers use the parallel-drive 'Centronics' interface).

The principles of serial data links are illustrated in figure 5.1, in which the pin numbers for the standard 25-pin 'D-type' signal connector are shown. The item of equipment (typically a terminal, printer or computer) at each end of the data link is termed a DTE (Data Terminal Equipment). The intermediate transmission path, including modems to convert logic levels to sinewaves and vice versa, is termed the DCE (Data Communication Equipment). Before a data byte is transferred from one DTE to the other, the following conditions exist:

(a) Both RTS signals are set low.
(b) DTR(20) must be set permanently high by each DTE. Each modem sets DSR(6) high if the data link is established.

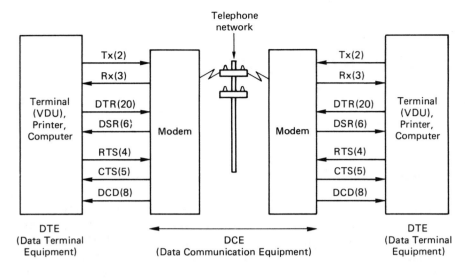

Figure 5.1 Generalised RS232-C (V24) serial data link

The following actions occur when a data byte is transferred, assuming that the data link is 'half-duplex' (bi-directional, but data transfer is in only one direction at a time):

(a) DTE sets RTS(4) high.
(b) Modem checks DCD(8) – if low, that is far end DTE has its RTS low, modem sets CTS(5) high.
(c) DTE sends ASCII character byte on Tx(2); other DTE receives on Rx(3).

In a full-duplex data link, both RTS signals can be set at the same time.

The local connection of a computer to a peripheral via a direct-wire link, that is with no modems and telephone network, requires that the computer 'emulates' either the DCE or a DTE. Figure 5.2 shows how the connections must be made for each arrangement. The advantage of (a), which is more common, is that straight-through connections, for example pin 2 to pin 2, are required. In (b) connection cross-overs are necessary, for example pin 2 to pin 3. To determine whether a computer is a DCE Emulator or a DTE Emulator it is necessary to study the device documentation, for example serial port pin functions, or circuit diagram. Alternatively the terminal can be disconnected and

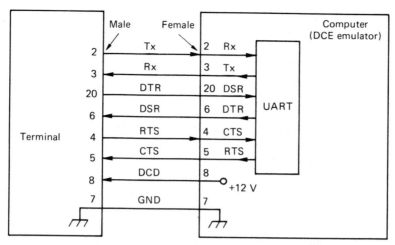

Note: TTL to RS232-C signal level converter between UART and signal connector is not shown for simplicity

(a) Computer is 'DCE emulator'

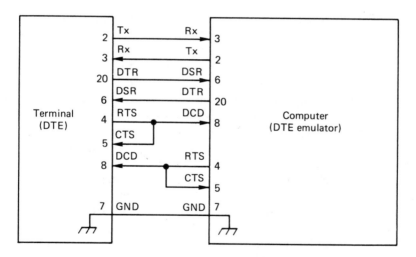

(b) Computer is 'DTE emulator'

Figure 5.2 RS 232-C connections for terminal (VDU) to computer

(a) if pins 6(DSR), 5(CTS) and 8(DCD) are at +12 V, the device is DCE;
(b) if pins 20(DTR) and 4(RTS) are at +12 V, the device is DTE.

(Note that RS232-C logic 0 is +12V.)

Frequently only a three-wire link is employed – 2(Tx), 3(Rx) and 7(GND) – and the control signals are connected 'back-to-back' at each end as follows:

4 to 5, 6 to 20

If a terminal fails to operate, it is worthwhile checking the states of the control signals. This can be performed with a DVM, logic probe or CRO, although access to the signal conductors is sometimes difficult. An alternative approach is to insert a 'break-out' box into the 25-way signal connector path. LED indicators on the box show the states of the relevant control signals, for example DSR should be permanently set (LED lit), while the RTS and CTS LEDs should change during the transfer of each character.

Clearly a common cause of the failure of a VDU to respond to an operator is the interconnection system itself, for example plug/socket connection loose or broken signal wire. Additionally the fault may lie within the computer circuitry or within the VDU itself. If a spare VDU is available then replacement of the suspect VDU may indicate if the peripheral is faulty. Therefore the interconnection system should be inspected firstly when a failure occurs. A replacement VDU could be installed, and normal operator commands entered to test for correct response on the CRT. Possibly only one-half of the overall input/output role of the VDU is operational, for example the computer displays characters correctly on the CRT but the keyboard is inactive. A simple technique for verifying VDU operation is to remove the computer signal plug from the VDU and to replace it with a test plug (female D-type) with pins 2 and 3 connected together. With this 'back-to-back' arrangement (Tx connected to Rx), the pressing of a key on the keyboard causes that character to appear on the CRT.

An ideal way of testing if the computer is sending characters correctly to the VDU is to enter a test program that outputs a single character continuously – the signal waveform for this character can then be monitored on the interconnection system with a CRO (oscilloscope). The test program can either be entered via another VDU in the computer system or can be held in a test-EPROM that can be entered on RESET or switch-on (see Chapter 4). A typical test program, written in Z80 assembly language, is as follows:

```
POLL: IN    A, (UARTCON)   ; Poll
      BIT   1, A           ;       busy
      JP    Z, POLL        ;            bit
      LD    A, 57H         ; ASCII for letter W (0101 0111)
      OUT   (UARTTX), A    ; Output on Tx
      JP    POLL           ; Repeat continuously
```

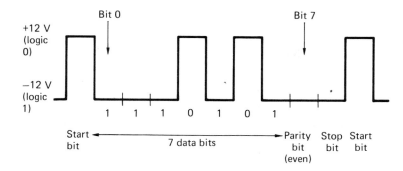

Figure 5.3 RS232-C waveform for character W (hex 57)

The waveform that should be observed on the RS232-C Tx data line is shown in Figure 5.3. The 8-bit character (7 data bits plus 1 parity bit) is framed by a Start bit (logic 1) and Stop bit (logic 0). Notice that the bit pattern observed (1110101) is in reverse order to that output to the UART (101 0111) in the test program. The UART adds a parity bit (assume that the UART is initialised to even parity) after the transmission of the 7 data bits. The characteristics of this waveform indicate the following RS232-C options, which should be compatible with the settings on the VDU:

(a) baud rate – each bit duration T = 1/baud rate;
(b) parity – even, odd or transparent;
(c) number of data bits – 5, 6 or 7;
(d) number of stop bits – 1, 1.5 or 2.

If no waveform is observed, for example permanent logic 1 (−12 V), the setting of the control (handshaking) signals should be checked.

The waveform on the reverse direction of the data link can be examined by placing the CRO probe on the Rx line, and pressing any keyboard key and the REPEAT key simultaneously. The RS232-C settings of the VDU can then be verified by examination of the waveform on the CRO.

The RC (Resistance/Capacitance) effects on long data links distort the pulses at the remote end of the cable link. This can cause failure of the receiving circuitry to detect pulses correctly. The easiest solution to this problem is to reduce the baud rate of the peripheral and the computer UART. Alternatively the 'current loop' option can be used in place of the voltage signals (on pins 2 and 3), and higher baud rates may be achieved. In this arrangement, current signals (logic 0 = 0 mA and logic 1 = 20 mA) for both Tx and Rx are transmitted along two separate pairs of conductors in each direction, as follows:

pin 13 – Tx + current
pin 25 – Tx – current
pin 24 – Rx + current
pin 12 – Rx – current

Alternative pin numbers may sometimes be used.

Faults within the VDU itself normally require access to the hardware/ service manual for the device. The general circuitry within a typical VDU and the overall principles of operation are described in Chapter 9.

5.3   Parallel printers

Printers connected to mainframe computers and minicomputers generally use RS232-C serial interfaces in order to reduce numbers of cable cores – as few as 3 cores (Tx, Rx and signal ground). Parallel printer connections generally require 12/13 cores. Microcomputers normally possess only one printer which is located at close proximity to the computer, and the cost of the multi-way interconnecting ribbon cable is insignificant. Consequently parallel-drive printers are generally used, and the world-standard 'Centronics' interface is applied. This consists (see figure 5.4) of:

(a) 8 data bits – pins 2 to 9 (pin 2 is least-significant);
(b) 1 signal ground – pin 16 (and pins 19 to 30);
(c) 3 handshaking bits – pin 1 (Strobe)
                                    pin 10 (Acknowledge)
                                    pin 11 (Busy);
(d) 1 paper low bit – pin 12 (PE).

Clearly the majority of problems that occur with printers are electro-mechanical in origin, for example paper jammed, ribbon broken, printing head (matrix or daisy-wheel) damaged or worn. However interconnections (plug/socket and cable) should be examined in the event of failure. An interesting failure symptom of an open-circuit in one of the eight data signal lines is that approximately 50 per cent of all characters are printed incorrectly. If no characters are printed the settings of the handshaking signals should be examined. The waveforms are illustrated in figure 10.2.

Various techniques are utilised in printers to produce hard copy of textual information:

(a) dot matrix – characters are constructed using a dot matrix pattern;
(b) daisy-wheel – a complete character is produced by a printing spoke on a removable print wheel;

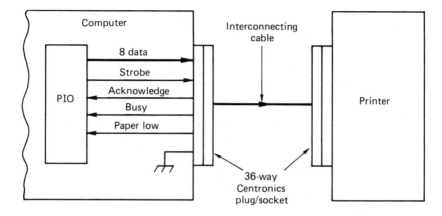

Figure 5.4 Computer to Centronics printer interconnection arrangement

(c) ink-jet – dot matrix arrangement;
(d) laser – fast, but expensive.

The first two versions are by far the most popular, with the daisy-wheel printer producing higher quality print characters – a computer applied for word processing applications normally uses a daisy-wheel printer. Matrix printers are faster in operation (up to 300 characters per second), and represent the most common devices used with personal computers – the design of a typical matrix printer is presented in Chapter 10. The great majority of faults are associated with the mechanical parts of the device. If a printer fails to print characters sent from the computer, the following checks should be made:

(1) Is the interconnection plug/cable/socket arrangement made?
(2) Is the printer powered up (power supply, fuse)? Is it set to 'Online'?
(3) The printer will not operate if the paper is loaded incorrectly – examine the 'Paper Out' LED, and reload paper if necessary (frequently a buzzer sounds when the paper is loaded incorrectly).
(4) Local ('Offline') operation of the printer can be tested, for example by switching the printer on with 'Linefeed' pushbutton depressed, causing a self-test print-out to occur. Additionally, operation of the 'Formfeed' (rolls paper up 1 page) and 'Linefeed' (rolls paper up 1 line) facilities in Local mode should be tested.

If these checks do not lead to successful printing, examination of the Centronics interface signals BUSY (pin 11 – set high to indicate that printer cannot receive data) and ERROR (pin 32 – set low to indicate various error states) may help to indicate the nature of the problem.

Failure to print characters correctly in either Online or Local modes is most frequently caused by the following mechanical failures:

(a) Failure of head carriage stepper motor or toothed belt drive – causes no head movement. Possibly a drive transistor to the stepper motor has failed. Alternatively the head PTS (Position Timing Control) optical sensor circuit is inoperative.

(b) Failure to print characters fully in a dot matrix printer (causing incomplete characters) may be due to the head gap being too wide, or one or more of the printing solenoids (typically 7 in a 5 × 7 dot matrix) or driving transistors may have failed. Clearly, incorrect loading of the ribbon cartridge should be checked firstly. If the fault is identified as a broken printing needle, then the head should be replaced.

(c) Paper feed mechanism failed – causes over-printing of characters on same row. The paper may not be fed correctly – the friction feed and sprocket drive should be checked. The feed may be jamming because of torn paper blockages. The stepper motor drive may be defective, perhaps because of a failed drive transistor.

(d) Broken ribbon. The ribbon cartridge should be replaced, ensuring that the pinion wheel engages correctly. It is possible to perform a temporary repair by opening the cartridge case containing the endless ribbon loop and rejoining the broken ribbon using adhesive tape.

The failure modes described above for a matrix printer apply equally to a daisy-wheel printer except that head replacement simply involves removing the daisy-wheel.

Unfortunately, routine maintenance of printers is not frequently carried out in most installations. This is despite the obvious inherent unreliability of the mechanical parts of a printer compared with other components within a computer system. The following routine checks should be made:

(1) Every 50 hours to 100 hours of continuous operation – inspect for ripped paper blockages, check for faint ribbon and correctly seated ribbon cartridge, and correct positioning of printing head.

(2) Every 500 to 1000 hours of continous operation – cleaning of all moving parts, lubrication of all moving parts (levers, shafts, teeth), cleaning of over-lubrication and accumulated dust, etc., adjustment (if necessary) of head position and examination of worn parts.

The simplest method of exercising the entire printing assembly is to run a self-test in Local mode. A full system test requires that the computer sends a test message, for example "The quick brown fox jumps over the lazy dog", or a more comprehensive string of test characters including lower case (small letters) and upper case (capital letters), numbers and punctuation characters.

5.4 Floppy disks

Floppy disks are used to hold programs in office and home microcomputer systems. A hard disk (or 'Winchester') is a non-removable variation of the floppy disk, and is faster, more expensive and has a larger storage capacity (up to 50M bytes) than the floppy. Most computer users are familiar with the handling of floppy disks, which have achieved their popularity because of their ease of use and reasonably robust form. However, mishandling of the floppy disk itself, for example dust deposits, demagnetisation and scratching of the recording surface, is a common cause of faults. In the event of suspected disk faults, the removable floppy disk should be replaced firstly to localise the fault to disk drive or floppy disk. Because of the complex nature of the drive mechanics and circuitry, it is customary for most users to return a faulty floppy disk drive to the manufacturer or distributor for repair. This is invariably the case with hard disk faults. However a simple cleaning operation of the floppy disk read/write head with a cotton bud soaked in an alcohol-based cleaning solvent may clear some faults. More complicated faults require an understanding of the operation of the drive unit and the data recording system used. This is presented in the following paragraphs. Additionally the operation of a 'bootstrap loader' program, which transfers the master program ('operating system') from disk into memory, is presented in Chapter 13 – this details the operation of a floppy disk control (FDC) chip.

Figure 5.5 shows the physical appearance of the three standard size floppy disks (called 'diskettes') the 8 inch floppy, 5.25 inch mini-floppy and 3.5 inch micro-floppy. Notice that the same features are apparent on the first two types, although the layout of the diskettes is different. Additionally the larger diskette is 'write-protected' by uncovering the write protect notch, while the smaller diskette is write-protected by covering the notch. The micro-floppy (or 'compact' diskette) has not achieved the same degree of standardisation as the two larger diskettes, and both 3.5 inch and 3 inch versions are avilable. It possesses the advantages of being smaller and more rigid, and the read/write surface is protected by a spring-loaded slider plate. The 5.25 inch diskette is the most popular for PCs, for example the IBM PC. The 8 inch and 5.25 inch diskettes should always be placed into their protective paper half-envelopes when not in a disk drive, to avoid dust accumulating on the recording surface.

Diskettes can be single-sided (SS) or double-sided (DS), and single-density (SD) or double-density (DD). The number of concentric storage tracks is variable, but is typically 80. Each track is divided into sectors of 128, 256 or 512 bytes. The start of each track is indicated by the detection of an Index pulse. This applies to a 'soft-sectored' disk; a hard-sectored disk, which is rarely used, has an Index hold at the start of each sector. The 'self-address', that is track number and sector number, must be stored at the commencement of each sector, because this is checked for each

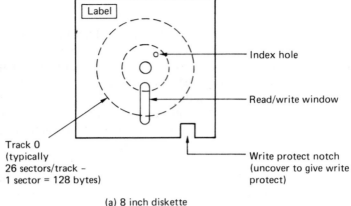

(a) 8 inch diskette

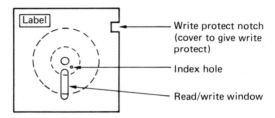

(b) 5.25 inch mini-floppy diskette

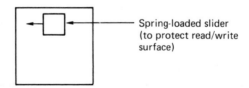

(c) 3.5 inch micro-floppy diskette

Figure 5.5 Physical appearance of floppy diskettes

subsequent transfer to or from that sector by the FDC. This self-address storage is achieved with a blank diskette by 'formatting' the disk; normally this involves the operator running a program called FORMAT. The specification for the layout of this self-address information, as well as data gaps between sectors, is contained in the 'IBM 3740 format'.

A generalised interface between a computer's FDC chip and the floppy disk drive is illustrated in figure 5.6. Data bytes are transferred in serial

CPU buses

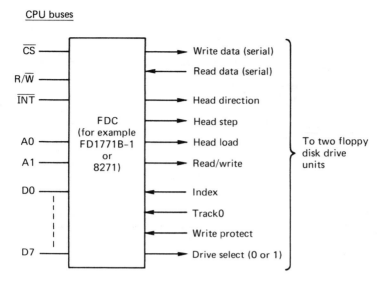

Figure 5.6 Floppy disk interface

form of course – the diskette rotates past the read/write head assembly which is positioned along a fixed radius of the diskette. Clock pulses are added to the data bytes by the FDC. The head is positioned over the required track using the Head Direction and Head Step (1 pulse per track) signals, which drive a stepper motor. The Head Load signal activates a solenoid which places the read/write head in contact with the disk surface during the transfer of sectors – a protective pad ensures that the surface is not scratched. The read/write signal selects either the write winding or the read winding – the latter produces an extremely small voltage signal which must be amplified in a 'sense' amplifier. The Index signal is produced from an optical detector (phototransistor) once per revolution of the diskette when the Index hole is detected. The Track0 signal is produced by an optical sensor (phototransistor) when the head is positioned over the outer track. The write protect signal is produced similarly by a LED/phototransistor arrangement when the write protect notch is uncovered. Clearly, inactivity on some of these signals can be detected with an oscilloscope, and may indicate failure of optical sensors or stepper motor. A generalised representation of the mechnical and sensor components of a floppy-disk drive are illustrated in figure 5.7.

The electro-mechanical or alignment aspects of floppy-disk drives that must be examined when floppy-disk failures occur are:

(a) dc drive motor (300 or 360 rpm) – frequently belt-driven;

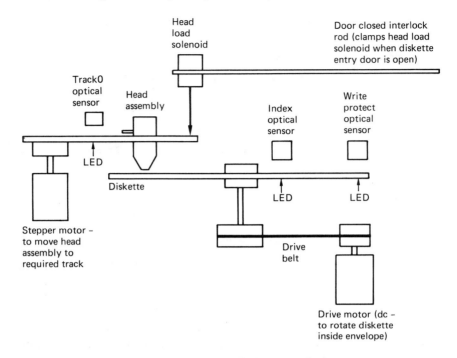

Figure 5.7 Floppy disk drive mechanism

(b) stepper motor to position head over required track;
(c) head assembly with read/write windings – head cleaning should be performed with care (avoid damage to head) using a cotton bud and alcohol-based solvent; alternatively a special head cleaning diskette can be utilised;
(d) various optical sensors – Write Protect, Index, Track0;
(e) head load solenoid;
(f) mechanical linkages, for example door closed interlock rod to (e).

If no obvious faults can be detected, a floppy-disk test program may be available to:

(1) step from track to track;
(2) read the contents of the control/status register within the FDC (see Chapter 13) – this can indicate the state of the various sensors;
(3) read (and display) bytes from disk;
(4) write bytes to disk.

It may be that mechanical adjustments are needed, requiring the use of an alignment disk which enables a skilled operator to make adjustments to the motor speed and head positioning. However, most faults with floppy disk systems are associated with electro-mechanical aspects and are caused by a fundamental failure of a mechanical or sensor component.

A typical sequence of checks that a maintenance technician makes is as follows.

Floppy disk fault checks

(A) Is fault localised to a single diskette? If so, replace diskette. Faulty diskette may be re-usable after re-formatting.
(B) Is drive motor turning? If not, check dc.
(C) Is diskette rotating within its paper envelope? If not, check drive belt (and clutch on older drives).
(D) Is head motor stepping? If not, check head step and head direction signals and Track0 signal.
(E) Is head loading? If not, check head load solenoid and door closed interlock rod.
(F) Is data read? If not, check Index signal and head read winding continuity.
(G) Is data written? If not, check head write winding continuity and write protect sensor.
(H) Is data failure intermittent? Clean head, and check alignments and motor speed.
(I) Is diskette surface damaged, for example scored radially? If so, examine pressure pad for trapped particles.
(J) Check interconnecting plug/socket/ribbon cable system between main-computer board and floppy drive.
(K) Check dc around PCBs in computer and drive.
(L) Attempt board changing, for example FDC board in computer and PCB in drive unit.

(*Note:* the sealed nature of a hard disk, or Winchester, device means that few tests, other than simple dc checks, can be made. It is customary to return faulty drives to the manufacturer.)

5.5 Audio cassette recorders

Low-cost home computers often utilise a normal domestic audio cassette recorder as a backing store device. Although magnetic tape cassettes are slow and possess small storage capacities, they are readily available and avoid the expense of a floppy disk drive.

The method of data storage is to convert logic levels (bits) into audio tones (sinewaves of two different frequencies) which are stored on the magnetic tape surface. The CUTS (or 'Kansas' standard) for audio cassette data storage specifies:

(a) logic 0 = four sinewaves/cycles at 1.2 kHz;
(b) logic 1 = eight sinewaves/cycles at 2.4 kHz.

The eight data bits within each byte are framed by a Start bit (logic 0) and two Stop bits (logic 1). This gives a transfer rate of 300 baud. A leader of 30 seconds of logic 1 and a trailer of 5 seconds of logic 1 should frame each block of stored bytes, for example a machine code program. Faster variations of this Kansas standard exist, for example logic 0 = one sinewave at 1.2kHz. Figure 5.8 illustrates the bit pattern and the sinewave equivalent for the standard Kansas (CUTS) waveform. Notice the similarity of the logic level waveform, which must be produced by the computer

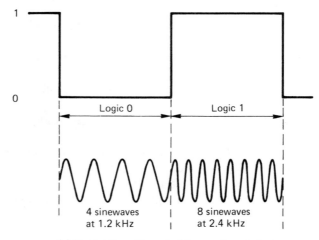

(a) Single-bit – with audio (sinewave) equivalent

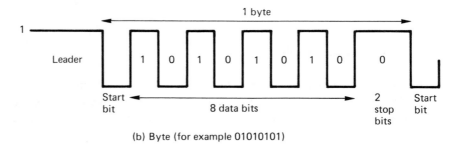

(b) Byte (for example 01010101)

Figure 5.8 Kansas standard for magnetic tape storage

circuitry, with the RS232-C waveform required for a serial data link (Figure 5.3). For this reason it is logical to use a UART to generate the logic level waveform (8 data bits + Start bit + 2 Stop bits), and to use the 0 and 1 logic levels to switch out two different frequency sinewaves to the casette recorder. However it is more common to utilise single-bit input and output port lines, for example on a PIO, as shown in figure 5.9. The motor on/off drive signal is optional. Software must create the Kansas signal when writing a data byte to a cassette, that is a pulse pattern of 1200 Hz or 2400 Hz must be generated, and the RC circuit rounds the pulse edges to produce a simulated sinewave. Similarly software must sample the data byte when reading from the cassette to detect each of the two frequencies in order to determine the logic level of each stored bit.

A typical sequence of checks that a maintenance technician makes when problems exist with a cassette recorder interface is as follows.

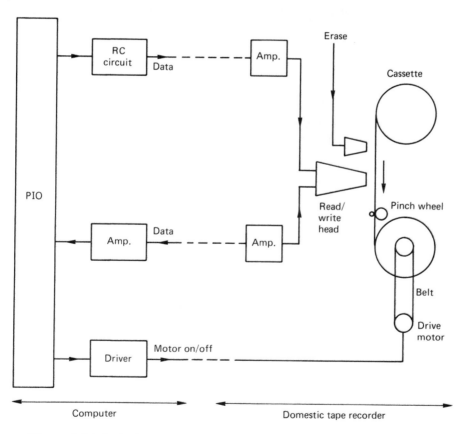

Figure 5.9 Black diagram of computer to audio tape recorder system

Cassette recorder fault checks

(A) Examine cassette tape; attempt a replacement tape.
(B) Replace cassette recorder (if a second is available) to localise fault to recorder.
(C) Check if motor turns.
(D) Is tape moving? If not, examine state of drive belt. Is cassette seated correctly? Is drive spindle rotating?
(E) Examine Read and Write signals between computer and tape recorder using a CRO or logic probe.
(F) Does tape read? If not, clean head. Check plug/socket and cable interface. Examine for broken read winding or faulty read amplifier.
(G) Does tape write? If not, clean head. Check erase head, write winding, write amplifier.
(H) Check head alignment (azimuth adjustment), and set the adjusting screw as required.
(I) If tape is stretched, damaged or subject to spillage, check pinch wheel pressure.

Bibliography

1. M. D. Seyer, *RS232 Made Easy,* Prentice-Hall, 1984.
2. M. Tooley, *Servicing Personal Computers,* Newnes, 1985.
3. R. C. Holland, *Microcomputers and their Interfacing,* Pergamon, 1984.

6 Signature Analysis

6.1 Principle of signature analysis

A signature analyser is a specialised item of test equipment that converts a complex sequential bit pattern at a circuit node into a hexadecimal 'signature' that is displayed on a segment display unit. This signature can be compared with a reference signature for the circuit node in order to help to identify circuit faults. The signature analyser is particularly useful for computer circuit testing. If a specific test program is run for a specific computer hardware configuration, then a repeatable set of signatures will be produced at different points in the circuit.

A common testing technique for an analogue system, for example a television receiver, is to monitor circuit nodes with a CRO (oscilloscope) and to compare the waveforms observed with reference waveforms. The signature analyser is a digital equivalent of this CRO testing system, and incorrect signatures can be traced through a digital system, for example a microcomputer circuit, until correct signatures are observed. The cause of the fault, for example IC or circuit connection, can then be localised. The great advantage of a signature analyser testing procedure is that the operator does not need a detailed understanding of the computer circuit or of the operation of the test program. He simply needs a circuit schematic and a reference list of correct signatures.

Figure 6.1 illustrates the physical appearance of a signature analyser. Essentially a signature analyser is a multi-stage (16-bit) shift register, and each 4-bit section drives one digit of a 4-digit hexadecimal display. The Start and Stop probes are connected to suitable points in the SUT (System Under Test), and the sampled signals at these nodes serve to open and close the shift register to the bit stream detected on the Data probe. The signal on the Clock probe is used to gate the signal on the Data probe into the shift register. A LED on the Data probe flashes when a bit stream is detected or when the signature is intermittent. Switches are available on the signature analyser to select rising edge or falling edge on the Start, Stop and Clock inputs.

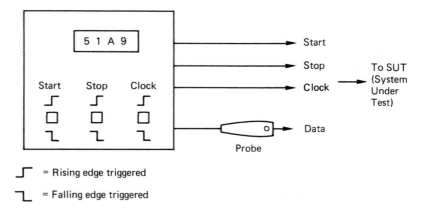

Figure 6.1 Signature analyser (front panel and probes)

Most signature analysers employ a different character set to the normal 0 to 9, A to F hexadecimal set, in order to avoid the ambiguity between the 7-segment representation for 'B' and '6' as follows:

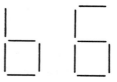

The character set chosen is 0 to 9, A, C, F, H, P, U. The choice of character set is unimportant because meaningful interpretation of a signature is impossible – a signature is either correct or not. The signature simply represents the residue in the shift register after a multi-stage shift operation on the signal observed on the Data probe. Several cycles through the 16-bit shift register are possible for most tests, and so the chance of inadvertently obtaining a correct signature when a fault exists is

$$1 \text{ in } 2^{16}$$

This gives a 99.9985 per cent probability of identifying a fault correctly at any circuit node.

The test procedure is as follows:

(a) Run a test program in the computer, for example a program that reads from every location in the memory map. This program could be held in a test ROM/EPROM.

(b) Connect the Start and Stop probes to suitable test points in the circuit.

(c) Connect the Clock probe to a suitable signal, for example the R/W control bus line.
(d) Connect the Data probe to various circuit nodes, for example IC pins, and compare the signatures observed with the reference list produced when the system was fully operational. Follow any incorrect signatures through the circuit until correct signatures are observed. It may be that correct signatures enter an IC, but incorrect signatures appear on the output pins, indicating a faulty IC. Possibly a circuit continuity fault, for example copper track or IC socket, may be highlighted. It may be necessary to employ a logic pulser and current tracer in the vicinity of the fault location, after this test is completed, in order to identify the precise failure.

Hewlett-Packard were the principal originators of this type of test equipment, and have set the standard for the test procedures used.

6.2 Design of signature analyser

A simplified representation of the operation of a signature analyser is illustrated in figure 6.2. Although not shown for simplicity, changeover switches on the Start, Stop and Clock inputs allow selection of triggering on rising edge or falling edge. The Clock input gates the signal on the Data probe into the shift register during the time window bounded by the setting of the Start and Stop signals. The segment display unit is updated when the Stop signal is set. Figure 6.3 illustrates the timing of signal waveforms, although a typical test involves a much larger number of Clock pulses and

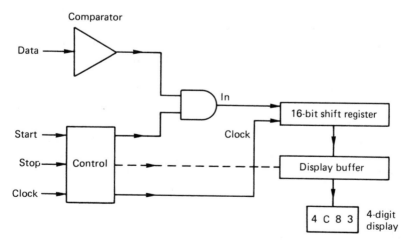

Figure 6.2 Internal operation of signature analyser

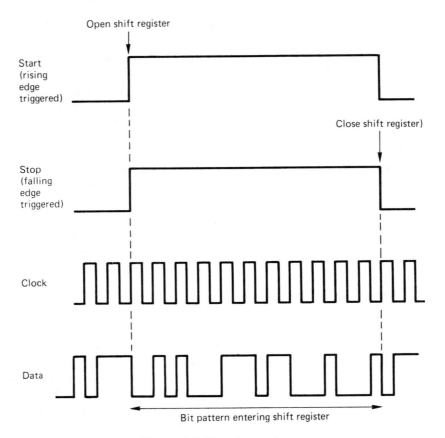

Figure 6.3 Signal waveforms

Data transitions. Notice that it is possible to use the same signal for Start and Stop – in this case the analyser opens the shift register on the rising edge of a suitable pulse signal and closes the shift register on the falling edge of the same signal.

The signature on the 0 V (Ground) line is always 0000. However the signature on the +5 V (Vcc) dc power line is variable, and depends on the nature of the test program that is executed and the edge-triggering selection on Start, Stop and Clock. However it is repeatable for each test, and together with the 0000 signature on the 0 V line it is termed the 'characteristic signature' for that test. These characteristic signatures are normally verified before circuit testing is carried out.

Figure 6.4 shows how a section of a reference list of signatures for one IC for a specific test is indicated to the operator.

The types of test program, and the parts of a computer circuit that are tested, are described in the following section.

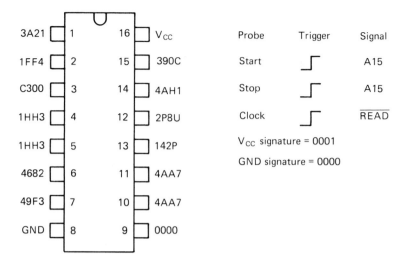

Figure 6.4 Part of reference signature list (one IC only shown)

6.3 Signature analyser tests

(a) Free-run test

This tests the system 'kernel' – see section 2.4. The computer is set into the 'free-run' mode by forcing the CPU continuously to obey the same instruction, for example a NOP (No-operation) instruction. Section 2.4 describes how this is implemented by clamping a fixed instruction opcode on to the data pins of the CPU. The CPU then steps through the full memory range of the computer, obeying the same instruction at each location, and the address lines change at varying frequencies (reducingly lower frequencies as address lines become more significant). Figure 6.5 shows the hardware arrangement. Start and Stop are both connected to A15 and rising edge triggering is selected for both – the signal waveforms of figure 6.3 apply to this test. The Clock probe is connected to the R/W (Read) control bus line, which is set by each instruction as the CPU steps through its memory addressing range. Therefore the analyser's shift register is opened when the A15 line is set, and closed when it is set next – this occurs when the full 64K address field (for an 8-bit microprocessor) is accessed. The Data probe can then be connected to the address bus lines, and signatures recorded. Correct signatures indicate that the system kernel (CPU, clock circuit, bus connections) is functional. Additionally the operation of the address decoder circuit (for example 2-to-4 decoder, or 3-to-8 decoder) can be verified. Signatures on the data bus are not

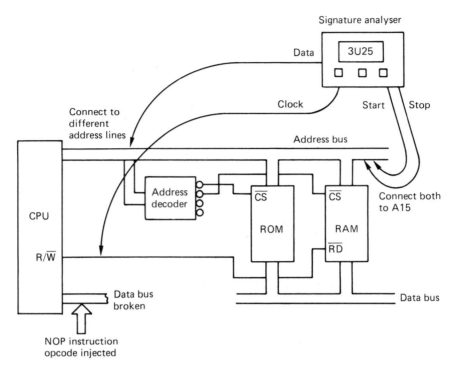

Figure 6.5 Connection of signature analyser to free-run microcomputer

predictable because of the random nature of information presented by RAM locations on to the data bus.

(b) ROM test
The same free-run test is repeated, but this time Start is connected to the ROM CS (Chip Select), with falling edge triggering selected, and Stop is also connected to the ROM CS, with rising edge selected. The Data probe can then be connected to any ROM pin, including any data bus line, so that the bit pattern is gated into the shift analyser's shift register only when the ROM is addressed. The bytes stored in the ROM are fixed, and therefore the signatures obtained on the data pins are repeatable and can be used to verify correct operation of the ROM.

(c) RAM test

RAM can only be tested using a signature analyser procedure if a fixed bit pattern is first written into each memory location. The test program can then read this bit pattern, and signatures will be repeatable. The Start and Stop probes are connected to the CS signal for the RAM, and the Clock probe is connected to the Read control bus line. This test program (for example write all 1s into every location within a RAM, read back this pattern) can be ROM-based. The Start-up ROM must then be replaced with this test ROM (see section 4.3) when a signature analysis test on RAM is required. Alternatively the test ROM could be entered by pressing a pushbutton that generates an interrupt, and the test program is held as an interrupt service routine in the interrupt space of the memory map.

(d) Output port test

Once again this test program is invariably ROM-based. It simply exercises an output port (or ports) by repeatedly writing to it. Conveniently it writes a different bit pattern consecutively to a port, such that successive port output signal lines are set. The Clock probe is connected to the Write (NOT Read) control bus line for this test.

(e) Input port test

The unpredictable nature of the data presented on to the data bus from an input port gives the same problem as reading from RAM. However if a bank of test switches can be connected as input signals to the port, repeatable signatures can be utilised.

6.4 Summary

A signature analyser test on a computer is very simple to perform. A test program is activated in one of the following ways:

(a) a free-run (single instruction) test is implemented on the system kernel, for example by replacing the CPU with a harness-mounted CPU supporting the NOP (or similar) instruction clamped on to the data bus;
(b) a ROM-based test program is entered, for example initiated by interrupt or by replacing the start-up ROM.

The fault location in the circuit can be quickly highlighted by the transition from good to bad signatures.

Signatures taken on the data bus for some tests are not relevant because of the unpredictable nature of data placed on the bus by devices such as RAM.

The smallest circuit modification will often cause a signature list to be inaccurate for a set of test programs. Clearly, a new set of reference signatures should be produced. Therefore there is need for accurate documentation covering circuit upgrades.

Bibliography

1. M. Slater and B. Bronson, *Practical Microprocessors*, Hewlett-Packard, 1979.
2. G. B. Williams, *Troubleshooting on Microprocessor Based Systems*, Pergamon, 1984.

7 *Logic Analyser*

7.1 Role of logic analyser

A logic analyser is an extremely powerful and flexible item of test
equipment for use with fault-finding procedures on microcomputer
systems. Although it is an expensive item of equipment, it can also be used
to test prototype microprocessor systems in a design/development function.

The logic analyser is a development of the simple oscilloscope. It
displays information concerning the SUT (System Under Test) on a CRT.
It is similar in function to a storage oscilloscope, because it 'captures' a
block of information (which it stores within its own RAM) which can
subsequently be displayed in a variety of forms.

Logic analysers offer a range of facilities, which tend to place them into
one of two different categories:

(a) logic time analysers ('time domain analysers') which offer CRT display
facilities similar to an oscilloscope – signals are displayed on a time
basis from left to right across the CRT screen;
(b) logic state analysers ('state domain analysers') which display the
sequence of program instructions as they are executed within the
computer under test – program instructions are displayed in order of
execution from the top to the bottom of the CRT screen.

Most modern analysers offer a mixture of the two display modes.

A logic analyser commences to 'capture' information when its comparator circuit detects a match between a set of operator-selected signal
settings and an identical set of signals from the SUT. Figure 7.1 shows the
method of connection of a typical logic analyser to a microcomputer system
under test. The clamp that terminates the interconnecting cable system is
placed over the microprocessor in the microcomputer board, so that the
logic analyser is able to monitor signals on the CPU's address, data and
control buses. The operator uses his qualifying pushbutton array to select a
'trap' condition, for example he may select to trap, or capture, when a
particular memory address is detected on the address bus. He then

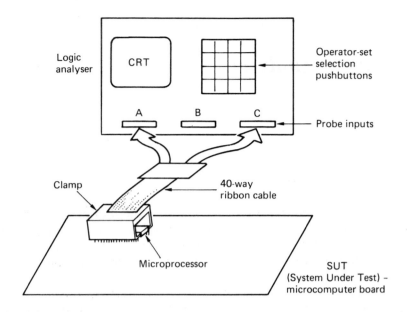

Figure 7.1 Connection of logic analyser to microcomputer board

subsequently uses further pushbutton controls to select the manner in which the captured information is displayed.

A different interconnecting cable, possibly also with an additional board inserted into the logic analyser, is used for a different microprocessor type in the SUT. Each replacement cable arrangement is sometimes called a 'pod'.

Modern logic analysers are sophisticated items of test equipment because of the range of display facilities offered, and they are themselves microprocessor-based (normally an 8-bit CPU is used).

7.2 Display facilities

An initial menu is offered which invites the operator to enter his required trap condition. This menu changes to the first of the display options when data capture occurs. The operator can then select further displays if required.

Figure 7.2 shows a timing analysis (time domain) display. This is the display format that was the only one available on early logic analysers, but is offered on modern analysers which additionally provide state domain displays described in the following paragraphs. The display is essentially that of a multi-beam oscilloscope. While a dual-beam oscilloscope is useful

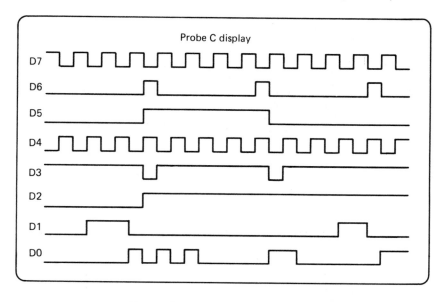

Figure 7.2 Time analysis display

for aligning two related signal waveforms; clearly a display of eight signals is more helpful for more complicated electronic systems. Unwanted glitches can be detected or time measurements on signal transitions can be made. It must be emphasised that the display is digital only (signals are sampled for 0 and 1 states only), and logic analysers are not designed to handle analogue signals.

Normally the state analysis display options are far more useful to the operator when testing a microcomputer system. Typically the operator selects a memory address that is accessed during a section of program which he requires to test. The analyser captures the information transferred along the data bus, together with the address bus setting, for subsequent bus transfers following the appearance of this memory address on the address bus. These data transfers can then be displayed in one of the formats illustrated in figure 7.3. The binary mode of (a) is a vertical (top to bottom) representation of the timing display of figure 7.2, but using logic 0 and 1 symbols. However it is of limited value normally. The hexadecimal display mode of (b) is more useful because it can be related to the fetch–execute cycle for each machine code instruction as it is obeyed by the program running in the SUT. However if the display mode of (c) is available, it is clearly the most informative, because it 'disassembles' the machine code program as it is executed. Normally the operator has available an assembly language listing of the program that is executed by the microcomputer he is testing. In the example illustrated he has chosen a

LINE NO	A BIN	C BIN
000	0000001000011000	01100010
+001	0000001000011001	10010000
+002	0000001000011010	11001000
+003	0000001000011011	00001101
+004	0011000000000000	10000101
+005	0011000000000001	00111111
.		
.		
.		
+015	0000001000101101	10100100

(a) Binary

LINE NO	A HEX	C HEX
000	0218	62
+001	0219	90
+002	021A	C8
+003	021B	0D
+004	3000	85
+005	3001	3F
.		
.		
.		
+015	022D	A4

(b) Hexadecimal

MAIN	ADDR	DATA	INST	OPERAND
TRIG	1800	R 3E	LD	A, OF
+001	1801	R 0F		
+002	1802	R 77	LD	(HL), A
+003	1900	W 0F		
+004	1803	R DB	IN	A, (80)
+005	1804	R 80		
+006	0F80	R 01		
+007	1805	R FE	CP 01	
+008	1806	R 01		
+009	1807	R CC	CALL	Z, 18E0
+010	1808	R E0		
+011	1809	R 18		
+012	1FFF	W 18		
+013	1FFE	W 0A		
+014	18E0	R 06	LD	B, 08
+015	18E1	R 08		

(c) Disassemble (for Z80 microprocessor)

Figure 7.3 State analysis displays

Zilog Z80 microprocessor 'pod', and the program is disassembled into Z80 mnemonics. The ADDR column on the display shows the setting of the address bus fed to the probe input A on the logic analyser, and the DATA column shows the data bus fed to probe input C. Additionally two control bus lines (RD and WR) are fed to the analyser (on probe C) and their states are indicated as 'R' (for Read) and 'W' (for Write) on the display alongside the DATA value. The display can be interpreted as follows:

(a) The trigger, or trap, address chosen was 1800.
(b) The first two bus transfers shown on the display illustrate the fetch–execute cycle for the first instruction (an opcode of 3E is fetched from memory address 1800, an operand of OF is read from memory address 1801). Subsequent program instructions require varying numbers of memory transfers in their execution.
(c) Line +003 shows a data byte being written into memory location 1900, that is the HL register-pair was set to 1900 before this section of program was executed.
(d) The data value read in from the input port (address 80) was 01 – see line +006.
(e) The CALL instruction transfers program control to memory location 18E0. Notice the return address of 180A being stored on the stack at locations 1FFF and 1FFE – lines +012 and +013. Therefore the stack pointer was set to 2000 before this section of program was executed.

The disassembly display option is clearly of value for testing new software. However it can also be of value when fault finding in the following situations:

(1) to monitor data bytes being transferred through input/output ports (or UART/CTC/FDC channels);
(2) to detect memory faults, for example data transferred unsuccessfully to/from sections of RAM, ROM-based information read incorrectly.

The 'captured' information can typically extend to 256 32-bit words, that is the logic analyser possesses 1K bytes of RAM to store the information following the triggering action. Each 4 bytes store one memory transfer – 2 bytes for the 16-bit memory address placed on the address bus, 1 byte for the instruction/data transferred on the data bus, 1 byte for control bus signals. Therefore several display screen pages of stored information can be examined by the operator. Additionally 'pre-triggering' can be selected, that is information before the trigger event can be stored and displayed.

One final display mode is available with some logic analysers, and this is illustrated in figure 7.4. In map mode, the analyser's CRT display represents the 64K memory map of the microcomputer under test, and

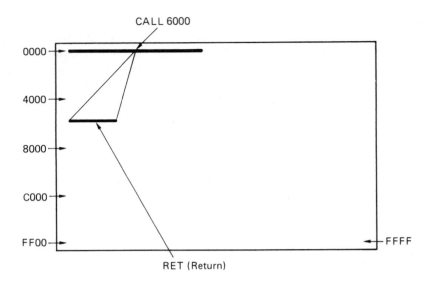

Figure 7.4 Map mode display

only the 16 address bus lines are monitored. Illuminated dots represent specific memory addresses, so that the display indicates where the computer is spending its time – the intensity of a screen dot increases as that memory location is addressed more frequently. For example the diagram shows that a program commencing at 0000 is looping continuously, and it is transferring control to a program section at 6000 – in fact this latter program is a subroutine in this example. The display can be expanded to cover a small area of memory in order to improve resolution. In this way program references to individual memory locations, for example data item storage to memory or transfer to input/output addresses, can be monitored. Although precise information of data transfers in a suspect computer cannot be gained in map mode (the data bus is not monitored), the test is useful in the following situations:

(a) in a free-run test, all points on the CRT should be illuminated (with equal intensity);
(b) execution of specific programs or subroutines can be confirmed;
(c) individual memory or input/output address usage can be confirmed;
(d) the map for a malfunctioning computer can be compared with that for an operational one;
(e) bus activity can be confirmed for inoperative computers.

Clearly, the use of a logic analyser requires that the operator has a more detailed understanding of a computer's operation than in the case of a signature analyser (see previous chapter). In particular, a knowledge of assembly language or machine code programming is essential if state analysis displays are to be interpreted correctly.

7.3 Logic analyser design

A simplified block diagram of a modern logic analyser is shown in figure 7.5. The comparator section detects the trigger condition, for example the operator-selected memory address is present on the SUT address bus. The 1K RAM that holds the captured information must be filled directly from the incoming signals from the SUT – the logic analyser's software is clearly unable to process the information fast enough. Details of each bus transfer (settings of address, data and control buses) in the SUT are thus stored directly into RAM, and the RAM counter is triggered by either the READ or WRITE control bus signal from the SUT. Frequently this RAM is circular in operation, that is it is filled repeatedly, so that pre-triggering can be used; in this case the analyser's CPU is notified when the comparator detects the trigger condition. The pushbutton array and CRT controller enable the operator to call the various display formats in order to examine the captured information in RAM.

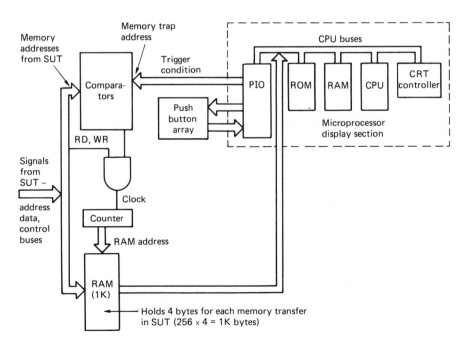

Figure 7.5 Simplified block diagram of logic analyser

The high cost of most proprietary logic analysers has caused many enterprising maintenance staff to design and build their own limited versions. Such a system, often termed a 'microbus analyser', is shown in figure 7.6. The comparator and RAM storage arrangement is similar to that of a full logic analyser, but the microprocessor-based CRT display system is replaced by 16 LEDs. After data capture, the operator selects memory addresses (and data items transferred) using the ADDRESS/ DATA switch and FORWARD and REVERSE pushbuttons to display the contents of RAM on the LEDs. The internal design of an even simpler 'data bus analyser' is shown in figure 7.7. In this system, the operator places a 40-way clamp over the microprocessor in the SUT and sets 16 address switches. When the analyser detects that chosen address on the address bus of the SUT, the 8 bits on the data bus update a two-digit segment display. Therefore the operator can observe the contents of each byte read from selected memory addresses. By toggling the changeover switch, the operator can observe bytes being transferred into memory locations also.

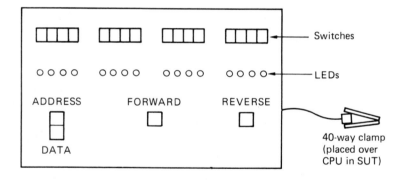

Figure 7.6 Microbus analyser

7.4 Proprietary logic analysers

Several manufacturers offer logic analysers, and the following devices are typical:

(a) Gould Biomation 9100-D and 920-D – timing analysis;
(b) Gould Biomation 1650-D – timing analysis and map mode;
(c) Hewlett-Packard 1607S – timing analysis and map mode;
(d) Hewlett-Packard 1615A – timing analysis and state analysis;
(e) Hewlett-Packard 1611A – timing analysis and state analysis and disassemble;

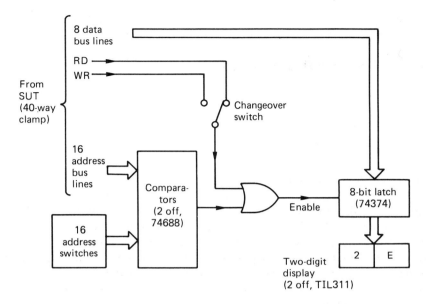

Figure 7.7 Internal design of data bus analyser

(f) Racal-Dana 211 – timing analysis and state analysis;
(g) Racal-Dana 200 range (201, 202 and 205) – timing analysis and state analysis and disassemble.

Tektronix and Philips also offer logic analysers.

Frequently a GPIB (IEEE 488) bus interface is offered, so that the logic analyser can be connected to a GPIB computer arrangement and system activity captured and displayed.

Additionally, some manufacturers offer boards that can fit into PCs (Personal Computers) to allow data capture from a SUT and subsequent data display on the computer's CRT.

Bibliography

1. M. Tooley, *Servicing Personal Computers,* Newnes, 1985.
2. G. B. Williams, *Troubleshooting on Microprocessor Based Systems,* Pergamon, 1984.

8 In-circuit Emulator

8.1 Development system

An MDS (Microprocessor Development System), or more simply a
'Development System', is a computer configuration that is used in the
design and development of microprocessor-based systems. An ICE
(In-Circuit Emulator) forms part of a development system. Although
primarily intended as a design/development tool, a development system
and in-circuit emulator can also be used for fault finding procedures on
microprocessor-based systems.

Figure 8.1 shows the hardware configuration in a typical development
system. The MDS is disk-based (hard disk or floppy disk, or both), and a
VDU and printer allow the operator to enter and produce hard copy of
different versions of a program under development. The program is
intended to be placed into EPROM (or PROM) for insertion into the
'target', or prototype, board. The target is a microprocessor-based circuit
intended for such applications as:

(a) cash register control board;
(b) industrial logger control board;
(c) telephone answering machine control board;
(d) washing machine control board;

or a host of other domestic, commercial or industrial systems. The control
program is entered in either a high-level language (such as Pascal or C), or
more probably in assembly language, into the MDS, and compiled or
assembled into machine code. This machine code program is intended for
programming an EPROM/PROM in the EPROM programmer. The
advantage of employing re-usable EPROMs, in conjunction with an
EPROM eraser, is clear for design and prototyping procedures. When the
final version of the control program is produced, it may be decided to
replace the EPROM with cheaper ROM equivalents for large production
runs.

The advantage of incorporating an ICE into the above design/
development cycle is that the repetitive process of committing the deve-

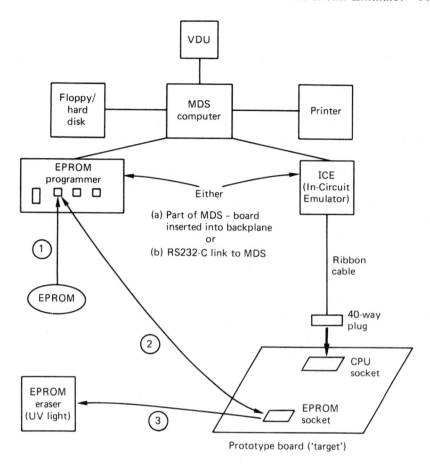

Figure 8.1 MDS (Development System) hardware configuration

loped control program into EPROM, and then erasing and re-programming the device after testing in the prototype board, is eliminated. The CPU is removed from the prototype board, and the flying lead from the in-circuit emulator plugged into its vacant socket. The operator can then test the control program within the MDS but incorporate sections of hardware (memory and input/output) within the prototype board into the test. In this way the control program can be amended and then tested using the prototype board any number of times, without committing the program to EPROM. The MDS is said to be 'emulating' (or simulating) the operation of the prototype board in this arrangement. At the start of an emulation process the operator will normally select that all memory and input/output addresses used within the control program use the MDS hardware, but then he can selectively choose the 'map', increasing sections of the prototype board hardware into his emulation testing procedure in place of the MDS hardware.

A different in-circuit emulator system is required for each different type of microprocessor supported by a development system. The ICE system consists typically of a PCB that fits into the MDS plus a ribbon cable and multi-way plug – this is sometimes termed a 'pod'. The ICE board is based on a microprocessor of the same type as used in the target. The specialised nature of an in-circuit emulator inevitably leads to a high cost, but its value as a development tool is considerable.

Clearly an in-circuit emulator system can also be utilised in a fault-finding situation. If the target is a suspect microcomputer board, its CPU can be removed, the ICE plug inserted, and test programs entered and run in the MDS to exercise parts of the suspect computer. A NOP test cannot be performed however, and therefore this MDS test procedure is of little value when the faulty microcomputer board is totally inoperative. However, simple test programs can be run to verify correct operation of memory and input/output circuits.

A development system can be put to one further use. It can be used to develop the fault-finding test programs described in Chapter 4. The programs can be emulated into a working microcomputer board, and then programmed into EPROM for use at a later time when a fault occurs in that (or a similar) microcomputer board.

8.2 MDS software

The MDS possesses an operating system as well as a series of utility programs to enable the operator to enter and test his control program. The operating system, which calls all other programs in the computer and manages the peripherals, is normally one of the following:

(1) *CP/M* (copyright Digital Research)
CP/M is used widely with 8-bit (Z80 and 8085) desktop computers. The ISIS operating system used in the Intel MDS is very similar to CP/M.
(2) *MS-DOS* (copyright Microsoft), or *PC-DOS* (copyright IBM)
These operating systems are almost identical, and each is often termed simply DOS (Disk Operating System). DOS is the industry standard for 16-bit and 32-bit single-user desktop computers, that is it is used for the IBM PC (Personal Computer) and its many clones/compatibles.
(3) *UNIX* (copyright Bell Laboratories)
This is the standard operating system for multi-user microcomputers, and is also used with many minicomputers. There are several derivatives, for example XENIX (as used in the Philips MDS), CROMIX and ZEUS.

The utility programs that support the operating system are listed next in the order in which they are utilised in the design procedure for a control program for a microprocessor application board.

(a) Editor

An editor is used by the operator to enter a text file. This is either a high-level language program or an assembly language source program in the case of a microprocessor development procedure, but it could be any document text file for other applications. The CP/M editor is named 'ED', and the UNIX editors are 'ed' (line editor) and 'vi' (screen editor). A word processor program can be used equally well, for example WordStar in a DOS system.

(b) Compiler/assembler

Compilers for the most frequently used high-level languages – Pascal and C – are commonly available in MDS systems. BASIC is normally an interpretive language and is not used for microprocessor system development. Program development is normally performed in assembly language, because of the control of input/output data handling that can be accomplished. The assembler is normally a two-pass assembler that allows the opertor to enter his program using mnemonics for instruction opcodes and labels (alphabetical names) for addresses (memory and input/output). Variations of a normal assembler are:

(1) cross-assembler – produces machine code for a CPU of a different type to that used in the development system, that is it cannot be run in the development system;
(2) macro-assembler – the programmer is allowed to nominate a name for a section of assembly language program, and the assembler inserts the equivalent block of machine code into the machine code file whenever that name is used in the source file.

(c) Loader

Many assemblers do not produce executable machine code. Instead they produce an intermediate 'hex' file, which can be directed to a printer or VDU to enable the programmer to read the machine code version of the program. The machine code version is expressed in ASCII characters, as shown in figure 8.2, that is each 4-bit hexadecimal number is converted into the 8-bit ASCII character code for that number. It can be seen that the final executable machine code file produced by the loader is approximately half the length of the 'hex' file (some additional information is held at the

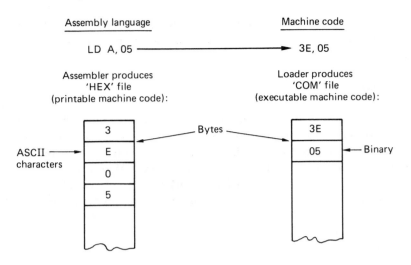

Figure 8.2 Files produced by assembler and loader

beginning of the hex file). The filename extensions used in CP/M and DOS describe the natures of these files, for example

Editor produces	FRED.ASM
Assembler produces	FRED.HEX
Loader produces	FRED.COM

Some loaders offer additional facilities, for example a 'relocating linking loader' which

(1) offers the programmer the opportunity to specify a different memory start address for his machine code program, that is he can 'relocate' it;
(2) offers the programmer the opportunity to concatenate ('link') two or more 'hex' files, which have been developed separately, together to produce a composite machine code file;
(3) performs the normal load function.

(d) Debugger

An alternative name is a 'trace' program. This allows the operator to execute the machine code program in a controlled manner in order to test for correct operation and to help to locate program faults. It also allows the operator to introduce varying parts of the target board into the in-circuit emulation procedure in order to exercise the combined hardware/software system of the prototype. Clearly, it also allows hardware testing of a microcomputer board in a fault-finding application. Its facilities are described in detail in the following section (8.3).

(e) EPROM programmer

The function of this program is simply to transfer the contents of an executable machine code file into an EPROM (or PROM). Normally a read-back, or 'verify', function is also available.

8.3 In-circuit emulator facilities

A debugger program allows a test program to be executed in a variety of ways and a series of checks to be made on the data processed by the test program. In this way a hardware fault in the target board can be examined. The range of facilities is typically:

(a) list the machine code program under test – this 'disassembles' the machine code and displays it in mnemonic form;
(b) display a block of data in memory;
(c) run to a breakpoint – stops the test program at a chosen condition (normally when the memory address of a specific instruction in the program is encountered);
(d) examine the CPU registers – the contents are displayed on the operator VDU;
(e) trace a specified number of instructions – obeys the required number of instructions and displays the CPU registers, as in (d), after each instruction;
(f) untrace a specified number of instructions – as for (e) but with no display feature;
(g) map areas of memory and input/output – select ranges of memory addresses and input/output addresses to be either in the development system or the target.

8.4 In-circuit emulation using the Philips MDS

Although a full MDS is an expensive item of equipment, several manufacturers offer systems to support one or more types of microprocessors. Intel were the first company to introduce an MDS, and termed it the Intellec system. It was designed initially to support the 8080 and 8085 micro-processors. One of the most powerful and flexible systems is offered by Philips, and a typical hardware configuration is illustrated in figure 8.3. A PC (Personal Computer) – an IBM PC or compatible – runs XENIX, and allows the operator to enter his test program in high-level language,

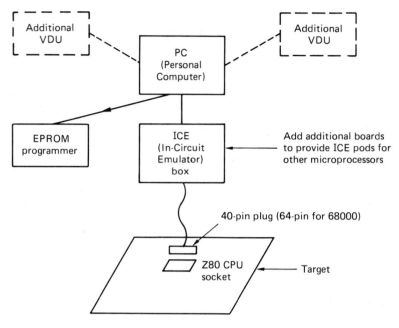

Figure 8.3 Philips MDS (development system)

assembly language or a mixture of the two. The in-circuit emulator box can support boards to provide emulation facilities for a wide range of microprocessors, for example

(a) Z80 8-bit microprocessor;
(b) 8086 16-bit microprocessor;
(c) 68000 16-bit microprocessor;
(d) 8051 8-bit microcontroller (single-chip microcomputer);

and several others.

Further VDUs can be added to the PC to provide a multi-user development system – several programmers can edit and compile/assemble their test programs, while only one programmer can emulate his test program into a target board.

The creation and testing procedure for a simple assembly language program that emulates into the target circuit of figure 8.4 follows. The program illuminates the right-hand display digit with the 7-segment pattern for the character '6' – a bit pattern of 10101111 is output to the segment port (to light all segments except b and p) and 01000001 is output to the digit port (bit 0 selects the right-hand digit; bit 6 must be set to 1 permanently for this particular circuit configuration). The debug procedu-

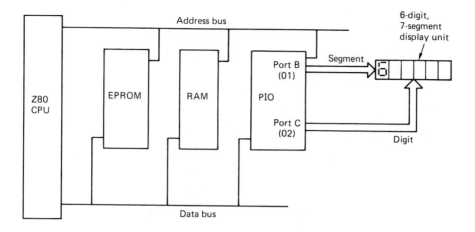

Figure 8.4 Simplified schematic of Z80 target for Philips MDS

re helps to exercise faulty parts of the target hardware in order to identify the precise location of the fault.

(a) *Log in*

```
login: stud1r
password: hello
```

(b) *Create File (Z80 Program)*

```
$vi prog1.s              Call vi (screen editor to create a file
                         named prog1. The extension '.s'
                         indicates an assembly language file.
a                        Append (insert following lines in file).
.sect write              First section of program.
.base 0x1800             Program start address (x = hexadecimal).
   ld   sp,0x1fff        Set stack pointer to last address in RAM.
   ld   a,0x90
   out  (3),a            Output hex 90 to control register
                         (initialise PIO).
loop: ld   ,0b10101111
   out  (1),a            Output binary 10101111 to segment port
                         (selects character '6').
   ld a,0b01000001
   out  (2),a            Output binary 010000011 to digit port
                         (selects right-hand digit).
   jp   loop             Jump to start of program.
esc                      To leave append (insert) mode of editor.
ZZ                       To leave editor and save file on disk.
```

(c) *Assemble Program*

    $z80 prog1.s   Call Z80 assembler (creates a machine code file name 'a.out').

    $convpmds a.out prog1   Converts a.out to prog1.

(d) *Debug Program (using in-circuit emulator)*

    $debz80   Call in-circuit emulator program.

    proc initp   Call procedure that specifies which blocks of memory and input/output addresses are to be in the target and which in the emulator (Philips).

    load prog1   To load the program prog1.

    run 1800   To execute the program from hex 1800 (the target segment display should illuminate).

    halt   To terminate emulation.

    quit   To leave debugger/emulator and re-enter XENIX.

(e) *Log out*

    Ctrl d

Note

Additional debug commands that can be used in the testing procedure are:

    mem 1800 1812 dis   To display (disassemble) memory; leave out 'dis' for data display.

    regi   Display contents of CPU registers.

    reset   Execute program from start (clear any breakpoints).

    tra + −13   Trace from top of screen listing to 13 lines forward.

    con tr0 d=3c=c=iow   Set breakpoint conditions (in this example tr0 denotes first breakpoint, data value of 3c, when input/output write occurs).

Similar test programs can be utilised to help to locate faults in microcomputer boards based on other microprocessors if additional in-circuit emulator pods are fitted to the development system.

Bibliography

1. R. C. Holland, *Microprocessors and their Operating Systems*, Pergamon, 1989.
2. R. C. Holland, *Study Notes for Technicians: Microprocessor Based Systems, Levels 4 and 5*, McGraw-Hill, 1984.

9 Typical VDU Design

9.1 VDU operation

A VDU (Visual Display Unit) is a computer terminal that acts as an interactive operator device. Information is displayed on a CRT (Cathode Ray Tube) and the operator enters commands and information to the computer through a keyboard. Connection between the VDU and the computer is via an RS232-C serial data link. Information can be displayed in text form (the normal typewriter character set) or in graphical form (colour or monochrome). In this chapter, a text-only VDU is described.

The information that is displayed is stored in RAM within the VDU circuit, for example in an 80 character by 24 line VDU a 2K RAM is required to hold the 1920 8-bit ASCII characters that can be displayed on the CRT. The use of this RAM highlights the difference between a computer/VDU arrangement and the system applied within a PC (Personal Computer). In the latter case the RAM is part of the computer's main memory, and is often called the 'video RAM' or 'VRAM'. A computer program (normally the operating system) places characters to be displayed in a reserved section of main memory, and a hardware circuit (based on a CRT controller IC) extracts this information and produces a video signal that feeds the CRT directly. Therefore there is no need for a serial data link, with UART devices at each end. However the use of VDUs is common with multi-user computer systems, in which several operator terminals are required.

A VDU control circuit is an ideal application for an 8-bit microprocessor. The microprocessor must interface with the operator keyboard and with a UART-based RS232-C data link to the remote computer. The control program must clear the display RAM on switch-on to prevent the display of random data characters.

9.2 Hardware – circuit diagram

Figure 9.1 shows a simplified representation of the VDU circuit, which is based on a Z80 microprocessor. There are three memory ICs:

106

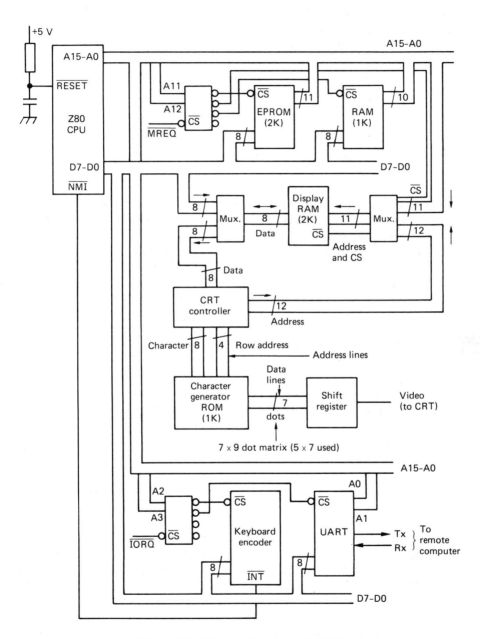

Figure 9.1 Circuit diagram of VDU

(a) EPROM – contains the control program;
(b) RAM – for use by the control program, for example for the stack;
(c) Display (video) RAM – contains the characters that are currently displayed on the CRT.

Figure 9.2 shows the memory map for the system and the way in which the dot matrix patterns for the ASCII character set are stored in the Character Generator ROM.

The principal task of the control program is to receive each character from the RS232-C data link and place it in the next free location in the Display RAM. The CRT Controller circuit examines these characters and generates the video signal in the following manner:

(1) 80 character-bytes are read out of RAM into the CRT Controller.
(2) Each of these characters is presented in turn to the Character Generator ROM, which contains the dot matrix pattern for each ASCII character – see figure 9.2(b). The character code is placed on the most-significant 8 address signals on the ROM, and the CRT Controller sets the 4 least-significant address lines.
(3) The same 80 characters are presented to the Character Generator ROM eight times to select each of the eight rows of dots required to construct the characters. The CRT Controller selects each row of dots by incrementing the 4-bit row address for each of the eight horizontal scans of the CRT by the electron beam.
(4) As each location in the Character Generator ROM is addressed, the required bit pattern for the row of dots is placed on the data lines. These are converted into a serial bit stream by the Shift Register to construct the video waveform that feeds to the CRT – see figure 9.3. Sync pulses are added to the bit pattern to form the composite waveform.
(5) When one line of 80 characters is constructed on the CRT, the CRT Controller extracts the following line of characters and processes these in the same way.
(6) This process repeats continuously to refresh the CRT. The cycle is only interrupted momentarily when the microprocessor addresses the Display RAM to write a character-byte that has been received from the RS232-C data link. When the microprocessor addresses the Display RAM, the address multiplexer is automatically switched to pass the microprocessor's address signals to the RAM address pins.

This entire hardware process of video generation is transparent to the control program. Its task is simply to place characters received from the data link into the Display RAM – the CRT Controller ensures that the CRT is updated with the latest list of characters.

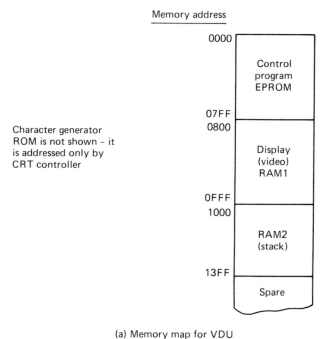

(a) Memory map for VDU

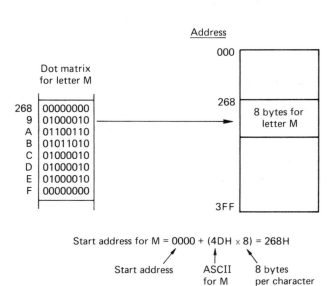

(b) Character generator ROM

Figure 9.2 Memory systems of VDU

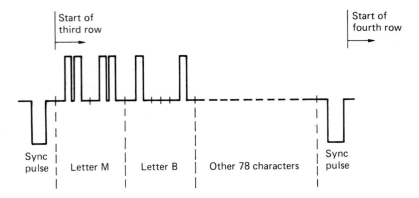

Figure 9.3 Sample video waveforms (third row of characters MB etc.)

The input/output addresses are:

Address	*Identity*
00	Keyboard encoder
04	UART Tx (transmit)
05	UART Rx (receive)
06	UART control register (to select RS232-C options)
07	UART status register (bit 0 is set to 1 when character is received on Rx, bit 1 is set to 1 when character is cleared on Tx)

The Keyboard Encoder is a special-function IC that is connected to the matrix of operator keys that comprise the keyboard – the column and row connections to this matrix arrangement are not shown, for simplicity. The device continually scans the keyboard to determine if any key is pressed. If a key is pressed, the Keyboard Encoder generates an interrupt. The control program responds to this interrupt by addressing the device, and reading an 8-bit code representing the key pressed into the CPU.

9.3   Software – control program

The control program is presented here using 'structured programming' and 'top-down' design techniques, that is the program is designed by defining its overall function and then breaking this down into structured modules. Each module is designed to be autonomous in operation so that its testing and ease of understanding/modification are simplified. In the case of an assembly language program, this involves breaking the program down into a series of subroutines.

The control program in the case of the VDU example presented here is more conveniently written as two separate programs:

(a) the main program, that receives characters from the remote computer via the RS232-C data link, and places them in Display RAM;
(b) an interrupt program, which is called by the keyboard encoder IC and reads in the code for the key pressed by the operator on the keyboard (this character is sent to the remote computer via the RS232-C data link).

Figure 9.4 shows the program structure using a block diagram representation of the program modules. In (a) the program, which is broken down into four modules, is named 'DISPLAY', and it consists of little more than four subroutine calls. These subroutines are the four modules, which perform discrete processing tasks as follows:

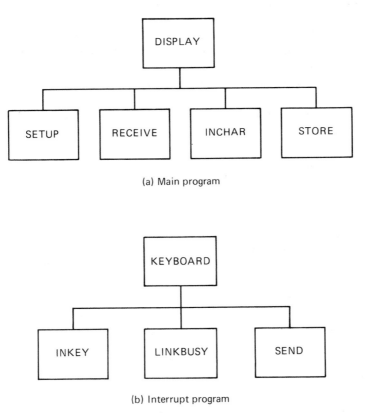

(a) Main program

(b) Interrupt program

Figure 9.4 VDU control program – top-down design

(a) SETUP. This initialises the UART to select the programmable RS232-C options (baud rate, parity, number of data bits, number of stop bits). Also it clears Display RAM to ensure that the CRT display is blank when the VDU is switched on.

(b) RECEIVE. This checks if a character has been sent by the remote computer – this consists of polling the 'character received' bit in the UART status register.

(c) INCHAR. This reads in the ASCII character sent by the remote computer through the UART.

(d) STORE. This stores the character received in the next free location in Display RAM.

The separate interrupt program (often called 'interrupt service routine') that handles the keyboard circuit is named KEYBOARD and is shown in block diagram structure form in figure 9.4(b). The three modules that comprise this program are:

(a) INKEY. This reads in the code for the key pressed from the keyboard encoder IC.

(b) LINKBUSY. This checks if the serial data link to the remote computer is busy – this involves polling the 'character cleared' bit in the UART status register.

(c) SEND. This sends the ASCII character to the remote computer.

The following is a simplified listing of the basic facilities in the two programs.

Program listing

```
;VDU control program
;This program controls a VDU circuit.
;It is divided into two separate programs -
;        (1) the main program that stores characters received from
;the remote computer into RAM
;        (2) the interrupt program that reads the code of the key
;pressed from the keyboard encoder.
;
;Main program DISPLAY
;This program receives characters sent by the remote computer.
;It places each character into Display RAM.
        ORG   0000H
  KEYENC EQU   00H          ;Setting
  UARTTX EQU   04H          ;          labels
  UARTRX EQU   05H          ;                    to
  UARTCON EQU  06H          ;                          input/output
  UARTSTA EQU  07H          ;                                    addresses
        LD    SP,13FFH      ;Load stack pointer with last RAM addr
```

```
          CALL  SETUP        ;Initialise UART, clear display RAM
    BEGIN: CALL RECEIVE       ;Poll UART until character received
          CALL  INCHAR       ;Input character
          CALL  STORE        ;Store character in Display RAM
          JP    BEGIN        ;Repeat program continuously
;
; ********************************************************************
;Subroutine SETUP
;Initialises the UART and clears the Display RAM.
;                 STRUCTURE
;BEGIN
;     INITIALISE UART
;     REPEAT
;          STORE ZERO IN DISPLAY RAM LOCATION
;     UNTIL DISPLAY RAM IS FILLED
;     SET UP START ADDRESS OF DISPLAY RAM FOR LATER USE
;END
;System outputs: UART control register (address 06)
;
    SETUP: LD    A, 3CH       ;Baud rate,parity,data bits,stop bits
          OUT   (UARTCON),A  ;Initialise UART control register
          LD    DE, 2048     ;Loop count of 2K
          LD    HL, 0800H    ;Start address of Display RAM
    LOOP: LD    A, 0         ;Clear A
          LD    (HL),A       ;Store zero in Display RAM location
          INC   HL           ;Increment address in Display RAM
          DEC   DE           ;Decrement loop count
          LD    A, D         ;Is loop
          OR    E            ;          count
          JP    NZ, LOOP     ;              zero?
          LD    HL, 0800H    ;Set start address of Display RAM
          RET
;
; ********************************************************************
;Subroutine RECEIVE
;Checks if UART has received a character from remote computer.
;                 STRUCTURE
;BEGIN
;     REPEAT
;          EXAMINE CHARACTER RECEIVED BIT IN UART STATUS REGISTER
;     UNTIL BIT IS 1
;END
;System inputs:  UART status register (address 07)
;
  RECEIVE; IN    A, (UARTSTA) ;Read UART status register
          BIT   0, A         ;Examine bit 0
          JP    Z, RECEIVE   ;Poll bit until it is not zero
          RET
;
; ********************************************************************
;Subroutine INCHAR
;Inputs ASCII character through UART.
;                 STRUCTURE
```

```
;BEGIN
;       INPUT CHARACTER THROUGH UART
;END
;System inputs:  UART Rx (address 05)
;
   INCHAR: IN    A,(UARTRX)    ;Input character to A from UART Rx
           RET
;
;****************************************************************
;Subroutine STORE
;Stores ASCII character received from remote computer into
;next free location in Display RAM.
;                 STRUCTURE
;BEGIN
;      STORE CHARACTER IN DISPLAY RAM
;      CHANGE POINTER TO NEXT FREE LOCATION
;END
;
   STORE: LD    (HL),A        ;Store character in Display RAM
          INC   HL            ;Increment pointer to Display RAM
          RET
;
;****************************************************************
;Finished main program
;****************************************************************
;Interrupt program KEYBOARD
;This program services the keyboard encoder.
;It reads the code for the key pressed, and transmits it over
;the RS232-C data link to the remote computer.
;
          ORG   0066H         ;Start address for NMI interrupt
   KEYENC EQU   00            ;Address of keyboard encoder
          PUSH AF             ;Store A and Flags on Stack
          PUSH DE             ;Store D and E on Stack
          PUSH HL             ;Store H and L on Stack
          CALL INKEY          ;Read in code from keyboard encoder
          CALL LINKBUSY       ;Is RS232 data link busy?
          CALL SEND           ;Send character to remote computer
          POP  HL             ;Reinstate H and L from stack
          POP  DE             ;Reinstate D and E from stack
          POP  AF             ;Reinstate A and Flags from stack
          RETI                ;Return from interrupt program
;
;****************************************************************
;Subroutine INKEY
;Inputs code of key pressed from keyboard encoder.
;                 STRUCTURE
;BEGIN
;      READ KEY CODE
;END
;System inputs:  Keyboard encoder (address 00)
;
   INKEY: IN   A,(KEYENC)     ;Input from keyboard encoder IC
```

```
          LD    B, A              ; Store character temporarily in B
          RET
;
; *****************************************************************
; Subroutine LINKBUSY
; Checks if UART is sending a character to remote computer
;                 STRUCTURE
; BEGIN
;      REPEAT
;           EXAMINE CHARACTER CLEARED BIT IN UART STATUS REGISTER
;      UNTIL BIT IS 1
; END
; System inputs: UART status register (address 07)
;
LINKBUSY: : IN    A, (UARTSTA)    ; Read UART status register
            BIT   I, A            ; Examine bit 1
            JP    Z, LINKBUSY     ; Poll bit until it is not zero
            RET
;
; *****************************************************************
; Subroutine SEND
; Transmits characters through UART.
;                 STRUCTURE
; BEGIN
;      OUTPUT CHARACTER THROUGH UART
; END
; Systems outputs: UART Tx (address 04)
;
    SEND: LD    A, B              ; Reinstate character in A
          OUT   (UARTTX) , A      ; Output character to UART Tx
          RET
; *****************************************************************
          END
```

Note

The program listing contains a large number of comments. These help to
make the program 'self-documenting', that is no separate program description is required to enable a programmer to understand and modify the
program. The 'STRUCTURE' statements follow the pattern of a high-
level structured language, such as Pascal, to describe the program flow of
each module.

9.4   Exercises

(1) The simplified control program listed here does not contain many of
    the additional features contained in a real VDU system. For example
    'wrap-around' is not applied, that is when the CRT screen is full an
    additional line of text overwrites the top line. The alternative approach

is to scroll the CRT display up by one line to accommodate the additional line at the bottom of the screen. Write down modifications you would make to the control program to implement 'wrap-around'.

(2) Assume that it is required to change the VDU from text-only to 'semi-graphics', that is graphics characters are to be drawn in place of ASCII characters in order to construct graphical displays. What eight bytes would you store, and where, if hexadecimal 30 is to produce a human face semi-graphics character in a 8 × 8 dot matrix?

(3) Write down the modifications you would make to the software to ensure that the operation of a CLEAR key (code hexadecimal 14) clears the CRT screen.

10 Typical Printer Design

10.1 Printer operation

The most common two types of printer are

(a) matrix printer, in which characters are constructed using a dot matrix (typically 5 × 7, in a 8 × 8 frame);
(b) daisy-wheel printer, in which characters are embossed on the ends of spokes radiating from a hub (the entire wheel is rotated until the character required is beneath the printing hammer).

In this example, a matrix printer is described. The printing mechanism is illustrated in figure 10.1. The printer head consists of 8 solenoid-driven printing needles, and the head is moved across the paper (80 characters wide) by means of stepper motor 1. A second motor (stepper motor 2)

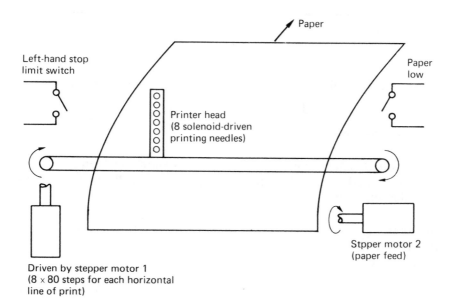

Figure 10.1 Matrix printer – printing mechanism

used to rotate the paper feed roll in order to move to the next line of printed characters ('line feed').

Two microswitches are applied to indicate:

(a) left-hand stop;
(b) paper low, for example no paper loaded.

The timing requirements of the Centronics interface, which is the world-standard for the connection of parallel printers to computers, is illustrated in figure 10.2.

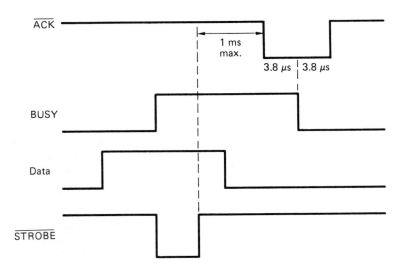

Figure 10.2 Centronics printer interface timing diagram

10.2   Hardware – circuit diagram

A simplified representation of the circuit is shown in figure 10.3. The system is based on a Z80 microprocessor, and two EPROMs are used to hold the following:

(a) control program, which is described in the following section;
(b) character look-up table, which holds the dot matrix patterns for all characters.

Four ports are required to handle all the input/output signals. Two 2-port Z80 PIOs could perform this task, but this particular circuit configuration employs a 3-port Intel 8255 PIO together with a non-

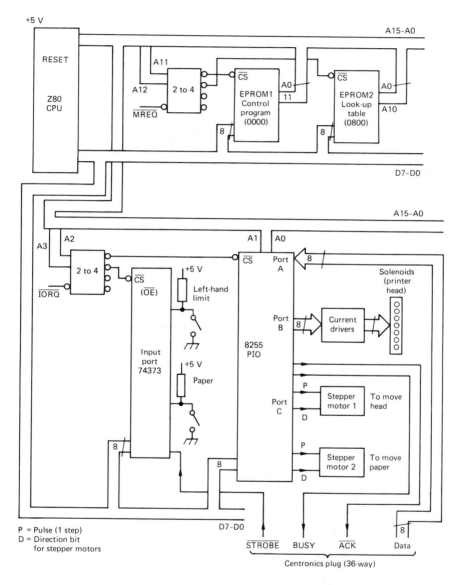

Figure 10.3 Circuit diagram of matrix printer

programmable TTL port (74373 8-bit buffer). The input/output addresses
are

Address	Identity
00	PIO Port A
01	PIO port B
02	PIO port C
03	PIO control register
04	Input port

Figure 10.4 shows the memory map for the system. Additionally the dot
matrix pattern for a sample character (the letter P) is illustrated. Notice
that the first byte in this 8-byte block is sent to the printer head solenoids

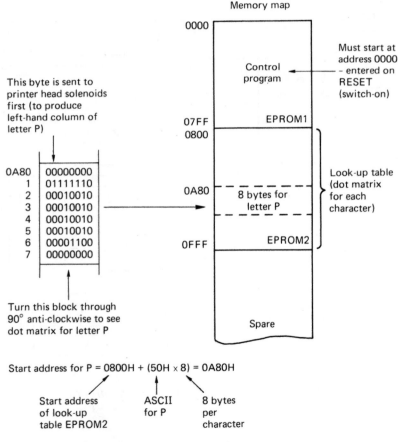

Figure 10.4 Memory map for matrix printer

first, to construct the left-hand column of the dot matrix pattern for the character P.

Note

The Centronics 36-way connector shown in figure 10.2 uses the following pin numbers:

STROBE – pin 1
Data   – pins 2 (least-significant) to 9
ACK   – pin 10
BUSY   – pin 11
GND   – pins 19 to 30

10.3   Software – control program

As in the previous chapter, the control program is presented in a top-down design. Structured programming is used, and this modularised program form is particularly beneficial in this case because of the relatively complex nature of the control program. Figure 10.5 illustrates in a top-down form the program modules. The main program modules (called as subroutines by the main program named PRINTER) are:

(a) INIT. This initialises the PIO (sets its port directions), sets the required
    initial states of the reply handshaking bits on the Centronics interface
    and positions the print head into the left-hand home position.
(b) RECEIVE. This receives (inputs) the character sent by the remote
    computer through the Centronics interface. This involves checking if a
    character has been sent and handling the handshaking bits.

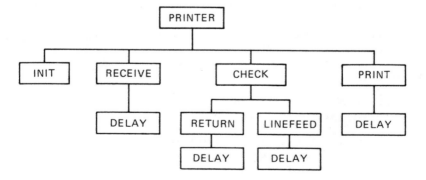

Figure 10.5 Matrix printer control program – top-down design

(c) CHECK. This checks if the character received is a special control character – Return (move the head to the left-hand home position) or Linefeed (move the paper up by one line). Nested modules (subroutines) are called to perform these functions.

(d) PRINT. This prints the received character. This involves sending the appropriate bit pattern to the print head solenoids for each column in the dot matrix.

There are three additional sub-modules (nested subroutines) that are used by the main modules – RETURN (perform carriage return on the printer), LINEFEED (perform linefeed on the printer) and DELAY (performs a variable time delay).

The main program is simply a series of subroutine calls.

Program listing

```
;Printer control program
;This program prints on a matrix printer each character when
;it is received through a Centronics interface.
;Main program
            ORG   0000H
     PIOA EQU   00H          ;Address of ASCII character input port
     PIOB EQU   01H          ;Address of head solenoids
     PIOC EQU   02H          ;Address of stepper motors, ACK & BUSY
  PIOCONT EQU   03H          ;Address of PIO control register
   INPORT EQU   04H          ;Address of switches and STROBE
            CALL  INIT
    LOOP: CALL  RECEIVE
            CALL  CHECK
            CP    0            ;Check if print
            JR    Z,NOPRINT   ;            not required
            CALL  PRINT
  NOPRINT: JR    LOOP
;
; ****************************************************************
;Subroutine INIT
;Initialises the 8255 PIO, and positions the print head at the
;left-hand side of the carriage.
;             STRUCTURE
;BEGIN
;     INITIALISE PIO
;     SEND HANDSHAKING BITS (BUSY & ACK)
;     MOVE PRINTER HEAD TO LEFT STOP
;END
;System outputs: PIO control register (address 03)
;                Centronics ACK (bit 0, address 02)
;                Centronics BUSY (bit 1, address 02)
;
    INIT: LD    A,03H        ;Control byte for PIO port directions
```

```
        OUT   (PIOCONT),A   ;Initialise PIO
        LD    A,00000001B    ;Bit pattern for BUSY=0, ACK=1
        OUT   (PIOC),A       ;Set handshaking response signals
        CALL  RETURN         ;Return head to left-hand limit
        RET
;
;***************************************************************
;Subroutine RECEIVE
;Receives an ASCII character through the Centronics interface.
;This involves transferring 8-bits of data and handling the
;handshaking bits.
;               STRUCTURE
;BEGIN
;     REPEAT
;           READ STROBE BIT
;     UNTIL STROBE BIT IS SET
;     READ IN ASCII CHARACTER
;     SET HANDSHAKING BITS (BUSY=1, ACK=1)
;     REPEAT
;           READ STROBE BIT
;     UNTIL STROBE BIT IS NOT SET
;     DELAY
;     SET HANDSHAKING BITS (BUSY=1, ACK=0)
;     SET HANDSHAKING BITS (BUSY=0, ACK=0)
;     SET HANDSHAKING BITS (BUSY=0, ACK=1)
;END
;System inputs:  Centronics STROBE (bit 2, address 04)
;System outputs: Centronics Data (address 00)
;                Centronics ACK (bit 0, address 02)
;                Centronics BUSY (bit 1, address 02)
;
 RECEIVE: IN    A,(INPORT)   ;Poll the
          BIT   2,A          ;          Centronics
          JR    NZ,RECEIVE   ;                    Strobe bit
          IN    A,(PIOA)     ;Read in ASCII character
          LD    E,A          ;Store temporarily in E
          LD    A,00000011B  ;Bit pattern for BUSY=1, ACK=1
          OUT   (PIOC),A     ;Set handshaking response signals
FINSTROB: IN    A,(INPORT)   ;Wait
          BIT   2,A          ;     until
          JR    Z,FINSTROB   ;               STROBE resets.
          LD    BC,0040H     ;Set delay count (for 0.5ms)
          CALL  DELAY        ;Delay
          LD    A,00000010B  ;Bit pattern for BUSY=1, ACK=0
          OUT   (PIOC),A     ;Set handshaking response signals
          LD    A,00000000B  ;Bit pattern for BUSY=0, ACK=0
          OUT   (PIOC),A     ;Set handshaking response signals
          LD    A,00000001B  ;Bit pattern for BUSY=0, ACK=1
          OUT   (PIOC),A     ;Set handshaking response signals
          RET
;
;***************************************************************
```

```
;Subroutine CHECK
;Checks if character received is a special control character.
;                 STRUCTURE
;BEGIN
;      IF CHARACTER IS 'CARRIAGE RETURN'
;           MOVE PRINTER HEAD TO LEFT STOP
;      ELSE IF CHARACTER IS 'LINEFEED'
;           MOVE PAPER ROLL UP
;      ELSE TERMINATE
;END
;
        CR EQU  0DH            ;ASCII
        LF EQU  0AH            ;       codes
    CHECK:LD    A,E            ;Place ASCII character in A
          PUSH AF              ;Preserve accumulator on stack
          CP   CR              ;Is it CARRIAGE RETURN?
          CALL Z,RETURN        ;Print it if it is
          POP  AF              ;Reinstate accumulator off stack
          CP   LF              ;Is it LINE FEED?
          CALL Z,LINEFEED      ;Print it if it is
          RET
;
;***********************************************************8****
;Subroutine PRINT
;Prints a single character.
;                 STRUCTURE
;BEGIN
;      CALCULATE START ADDRESS OF DOT MATRIX FOR CHARACTER
;      REPEAT
;           SEND DOT MATRIX PATTERN FOR COLUMN TO SOLENOIDS
;           MOVE HEAD STEPPER MOTOR TO NEXT COLUMN POSITION
;      UNTIL 8 COLUMNS OF DOT MATRIX ARE PRINTED
;END
;System outputs: Head solenoids (address 01)
;                Head stepper motor 1 (bits 2 & 3, address 02)
;
    PRINT:LD   HL,0800H        ;Start address of look-up table
          SLA  E               ;Shift ASCII character left
          SLA  E               ;Three shifts
          SLA  E               ;           multiply by 8
          LD   D,0             ;Clear D
          ADD  HL,DE           ;Start address = 0800 + ASCII*8
          LD   D,8             ;Loop count (8 columns in dot matrix)
    MATRIX:LD   A,(HL)         ;Fetch byte for dot matrix
          OUT  (PIOB),A        ;Send to head solenoids
          LD   A,00000101B     ;Bit pattern for pulse start
          OUT  (PIOC),A        ;Send to stepper motor 1
          LD   BC,03FFH        ;Set delay count (for 10ms)
          CALL DELAY           ;Delay
          LD   A,00000001B     ;Bit pattern for pulse end
          OUT  (PIOC),A        ;Send to stepper motor 1
          LD   BC,03FFH        ;Set delay count (for 10ms)
```

```
        CALL DELAY          ;Delay
        INC  HL             ;Step to next column in dot matrix
        DEC  D              ;Repeat loop
        JR   NZ,MATRIX      ;              8 times
        RET
;
;Completed the main modules (subroutines) INIT, RECEIVE,
;CHECK and PRINT
;Now for the sub-modules (nested subroutines).
;
;****************************************************************
;Subroutine RETURN
;Moves the printer head back to the left-hand edge of paper.
;               STRUCTURE
;BEGIN
;      IF LEFT-HAND LIMIT SWITCH IS NOT SET
;           MOVE HEAD STEPPER MOTOR TO LEFT
;      ELSE
;           TERMINATE
;END
;System inputs:  Left-hand limit switch (bit 0, address 04)
;System outputs: Head stepper motor 1 (bits 2 & 3, address 02)
;
  RETURN: IN   A,(INPORT)    ;Read input port
          BIT  0,A           ;Is left-hand limit
          RET  Z             ;               switch set?
          LD   A,00001101B   ;Bit pattern for pulse start
          OUT  (PIOC),A      ;Send to stepper motor 1
          LD   BC,03FFH      ;Set delay count (for 10 ms)
          CALL DELAY         ;Delay
          LD   A,00001001B   ;Bit pattern for pulse end
          OUT  (PIOC),A      ;Send to stepper motor 1
          LD   BC,03FFH      ;Set delay count (for 10 ms)
          CALL DELAY         ;Delay
          JR   RETURN        ;Repeat
;
;****************************************************************
;Subroutine LINEFEED
;Moves the paper roll up by one printing line.
;               STRUCTURE
;BEGIN
;      PULSE PAPER FEED STEPPER MOTOR
;END
;System outputs: Paper stepper motor 2 (bits 4 & 5, address 02)
;
LINEFFED: LD   A,00010001B   ;Bit pattern for pulse start
          OUT  (PIOC),A      ;Send to stepper motor 2
          LD   BC,03FFH      ;Set delay count (for 10 ms)
          CALL DELAY         ;Delay
          LD   A,00000001B   ;Bit pattern for pulse end
          OUT  (PIOC),A      ;Send to stepper motor 2
          LD   BC,03FFH      ;Set delay count (for 10 ms)
```

```
        CALL  DELAY        ;Delay
        LD    A, 0         ;Set flag for no printing required
        RET
;
;***************************************************************
;Subroutine DELAY
;Produces a variable delay, based on delay count in BC.
;              STRUCTURE
;BEGIN
;    REPEAT
;         DECREMENT DELAY COUNT IN BC
;    UNTIL BC EQUALS 0
;END
;
    DELAY: DEC  BC         ;Decrement register-pair
           LD   A, B       ;Transfer B to A
           OR   C          ;Are A and C the same (zero)?
           JR   NZ, DELAY  ;Repeat if not
           RET
;***************************************************************
           END
```

10.4   Exercises

(1) For simplicity, the circuit diagram and the control program did not use a stack. Clearly this is necessary because subroutine CALL instructions are used. What additions are necessary to the hardware and software to incorporate a stack?

(2) Some printers designed for the US market produce the # symbol in place of the £ symbol (used for the UK market) for ASCII code hex 23. If you were required to adapt a US printer to a UK printer, write down the bit pattern you would choose for this character. Additionally, calculate the start address of the data block in memory that requires to be altered to hold the dot matrix pattern for this character.

(3) Sketch the additional circuitry required if the printer is to sound a bell when the ASCII character 'BEL' is received.

(4) Assume that the printer is to be converted to print Arabic characters. Would you agree that EPROM2 (the character look-up table) needs to be changed? An additional modification needs to be made to ensure that the print head moves from right to left (Arabic characters are drawn in the reverse direction to European characters). Describe how could this be performed by:

(a) hardware, using a single-bit inverter;
(b) software, changing only 4 instructions.

(5) The control program does not contain a section to handle the 'Paper Low' microswitch shown in the circuit diagram. Write down the modifications and additions you would make to the control program to handle this signal. The ACK handshaking signal to the remote computer should not be set if the paper is low, the character should not be printed and an additional handshaking response signal (bit 6, address 02) should be set high on the Centronics interface return to the remote computer.

(6) Consider how other features that are available on commercial printers could be included. Such features are:

   (a) manual pushbuttons to give local manual control of such features as Form Feed (move paper up through 1 page) and Linefeed;
   (b) self-test (triggered manually);
   (c) use of a line buffer, such that head prints one line of characters during its travel from left to right, and another line of characters during its travel from right to left (flyback).

11 Typical EPROM Programmer Design

11.1 EPROM programming

EPROMs are used widely to hold short programs or data lists in applications in which the stored information may occasionally be required to be changed. A 20-minute erasure time under a UV light source clears the EPROM, and the device can then be reprogrammed.

EPROMs are avilable in the following memory sizes (the digits after '27' denote the number of stored bits in units of 1K bits):

> 2708 – 1K × 8 (1024 locations, 8 bits per location)
> 2716 – 2K × 8 (2048 locations, 8 bits per location)
> 2732 – 4K × 8 (4096 locations, 8 bits per location)
> etc.

Probably the most popular device is the 2716, since 2K bytes is a memory capacity that is sufficient for a wide range of applications. Its pin functions are illustrated in figure 11.1, and the timing diagrams for its interconnecting signals, during initial programming and when it is addressed in its final circuit, are shown in figure 11.2

EPROM programmers are available in two primary forms:

(a) as small stand-alone microcomputers – the required information is entered via a manual keyboard into RAM, and when programming occurs this information is transferred a byte at a time into EPROM; alternatively the information is transferred from a larger computer system by RS232-C serial data link into the system RAM;
(b) as additional hardware and software facilities within an MDS (Microprocessor Development System) – an assembly language source file is converted to a machine code file on disk, and this latter file is transferred a byte at a time into EPROM.

11.2 Hardware – circuit diagram

The simplified circuit diagram of a stand-alone EPROM programmer, which incorporates manual entry of required information, is shown in

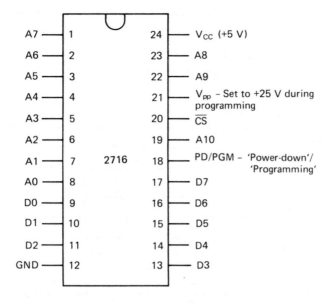

Figure 11.1 2716 EPROM pin functions

figure 11.3. The operator enters bytes into RAM1 using the three-position switch LOWER/UPPER/DATA to select:

(a) lower half of memory address;
(b) upper half of memory address;
(c) data byte;

in conjunction with the eight data switches and the ENTER pushbutton. When the operator has entered all required bytes, he presses the PRO-GRAM pushbutton in order to transfer the contents of RAM1 into the blank EPROM placed in the ZIF (Zero Insertion Force) socket. An example of the method the operator uses to specify that a byte of A3 is to be stored in EPROM address 014D is:

(1) Set 4D on 8 data switches. Set LOWER/UPPER/DATA to
     LOWER.
     Press ENTER.
(2) Set 01 on 8 data switches. Set LOWER/UPPER/DATA to UPPER.
     Press ENTER.
(3) Set A3 on 8 data switches. Set LOWER/UPPER/DATA to DATA.
     Press ENTER.

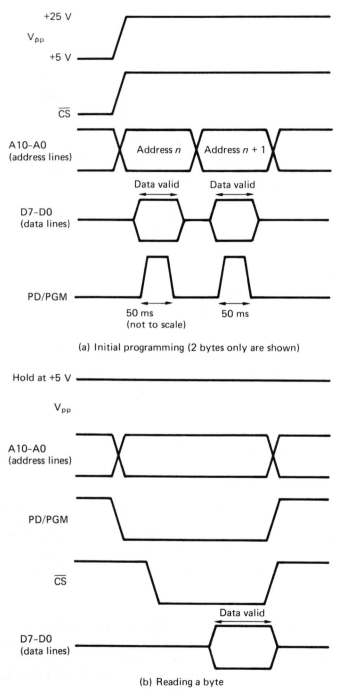

(a) Initial programming (2 bytes only are shown)

(b) Reading a byte

Figure 11.2 2716 EPROM signal timing

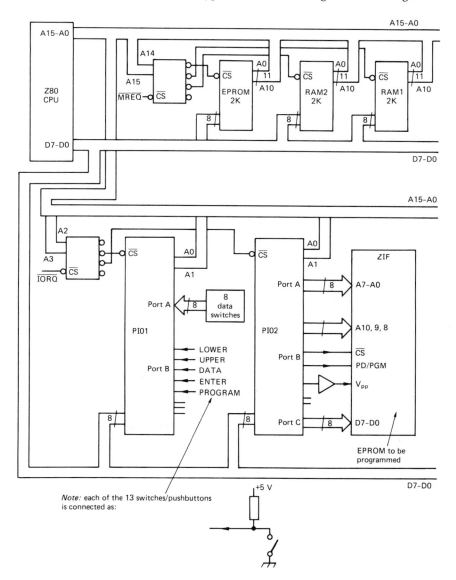

Figure 11.3 Circuit diagram of EPROM programmer

The control program is held in the EPROM, and RAM2 is for use by the control program, for example for the stack – the memory map for the system is shown in figure 11.4. The EPROM to be programmed is placed in the ZIF socket – the operation of a clamping lever secures the legs of the EPROM IC. The address, data and control signals to the EPROM to be programmed are generated by PIO2.

Memory address

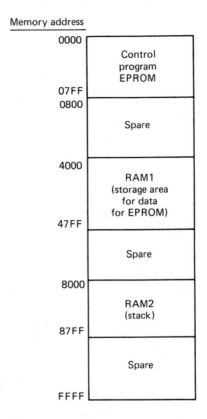

Figure 11.4 Memory map for EPROM programmer

The input/output addresses are:

Address	Identity
04	PIO1 port A
05	PIO1 port B
06	PIO1 port C
07	PIO1 control register
08	PIO2 port A
09	PIO2 port B
0A	PIO2 port C
0B	PIO2 control register

For simplicity, no numerical display, for example segment display, to guide the operator during entry procedure, is shown.

11.3 Software – control program

Figure 11.5 shows the modules used in the control program. The main program EPROM simply calls the two modules (subroutines) INIT and INPUT. There are further levels of nesting from INPUT. The modules perform the following functions:

(a) INIT. This initialises (selects the port directions) PI01 and PI02.
(b) INPUT. This checks whether the ENTER or PROGRAM pushbuttons are pressed. If ENTER is pressed the subroutine READ is called, and if PROGRAM is pressed the subroutine PROGRAM is called.
(c) READ. This reads in operator entries of address and data into RAM for later transfer to EPROM. The operator uses the 8 data switches as well as the three-position LOWER/UPPER/DATA switch.
(d) PROGRAM. This transfers 2K bytes from RAM into the EPROM placed in the ZIF socket. The programming of each byte takes 50 ms.
(e) DELAY. This generates a time delay of 50 ms for use by the PROGRAM module.

Note

The software method applied in the following program listing to read the settings of the ENTER and PROGRAM pushbuttons is simplified. Normally software techniques are applied to avoid reading the operation of a pushbutton several times before its release by the operator and to eliminate the effects of contact bounce. In this system these measures are not essential.

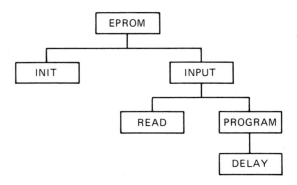

Figure 11.5 EPROM programmer control program – top-down design

Program listing

```
;EPROM programmer control program.
;This program allows the operator to enter program/data into RAM,
;and this information can then be transferred to EPROM.
;Main program
            ORG    0000H
    PIO1A EQU    04H          ;8 data switches
    PIO1B EQU    05H          ;2 push buttons, 3-position switch
    PIO1C EQU    06H          ;Not used
PIO1CONT EQU    07H          ;Control register for PIO1
    PIO2A EQU    08H          ;Address pins (8) on EPROM
    PIO2B EQU    09H          ;Address (3) on EPROM + CS, PD/PGM, Vpp
    PIO2C EQU    0AH          ;Data pins on EPROM
PIO2CONT EQU    0BH          ;Control register for PIO2
            LD     SP, 87FFH    ;Set stack pointer to end of RAM2
            CALL   INIT         ;Initialise PIOs
    REPEAT: CALL   INPUT        ;Check operation of keys
            JP     REPEAT
;
;****************************************************************
;Subroutine INIT
;Initialises PIO1 and PIO2
;               STRUCTURE
;BEGIN
;       INITIALISE PIO1
;       INITIALISE PIO2
;END
;System outputs: PIO1 control register (address 07)
;                PIO2 control register (address 0B)
;
      INIT: LD     A, 02H       ;Control byte for PIO1 port directions
            OUT    (PIO1CONT), A ;Send to control register
            LD     A, 42H       ;Control byte for PIO2 port directions
            OUT    (PIO2CONT), A ;Send to control register
            RET
;
;****************************************************************
;Subroutine INPUT
;Reads the pushbuttons (ENTER and PROGRAM), and calls READ
; (operator entry of EPROM address and data byte), or PROGRAM
; (transfer 2K bytes to EPROM) as necessary.
;               STRUCTURE
;BEGIN
;       SET RAM1 START ADDRESS
;       IF ENTER PUSHBUTTON IS PRESSED
;               CALL READ MODULE (READS IN BYTE)
;       ELSE IF PROGRAM PUSHBUTTON IS PRESSED
;               CALL PROGRAM MODULE (PROGRAMS EPROM)
;       ELSE TERMINATE
;END
;System inputs:  ENTER pushbutton (address 05, bit 3)
```

```
;                    PROGRAM pushbutton (address 05, bit 4)
;                    3-position switch (address 05, bits 0 to 2)
   INPUT:LD    HL,4000H        ;Start address of RAM1
         IN    A,(PIO1B)       ;Read pushbuttons and switches
         BIT   3,A             ;Check ENTER pushbutton
         CALL  Z,READ          ;Call READ if ENTER is pressed
         IN    A,(PIO1B)       ;Read pushbuttons and switches
         BIT   4,A             ;Check PROGRAM pushbutton
         CALL  Z,PROGRAM       ;Call PROGRAM if pushbutton is pressed
         RET
;
;****************************************************************
;This reads the switches when ENTER is pressed.  It handles the
;operator's entries of address (places it into BC) and data
;(places it into RAM1) for the EPROM.
;                 STRUCTURE
;BEGIN
;    IF LOWER SWITCH IS SET
;         READ 8 DATA SWITCHES AS LOWER HALF OF ADDRESS
;    ELSE IF UPPER SWITCH IS SET
;         READ 8 DATA SWITCHES AS UPPER HALF OF ADDRESS
;    ELSE
;         READ 8 DATA SWITCHES AS DATA
;         STORE DATA IN RAM1
;END
;System inputs:  8 data switches (address 04)
;                3-position switch (LOWER - address 05, bit 0
;                                   UPPER - address 05, bit 1
;                                   DATA  - address 05, bit 2)
;
   READ:BIT   0,A              ;Check bit 0 - LOWER switch
        JP    NZ,NOTLOW        ;Jump if LOWER is not set
        IN    A,(PIO1A)        ;Read settings of 8 data switches
        LD    C,A              ;Store in C (part of BC)
        JP    COMPLETE
 NOTLOW:BIT   1,A              ;Check bit 1 - UPPER switch
        JP    NZ,NOTHIGH       ;Jump if UPPER is not set
        IN    A,(PIO1A)        ;Read settings of 8 data switches
        LD    B,A              ;Store in B (part of BC)
        JP    COMPLETE
NOTHIGH:IN    A,(PIO1A)        ;Read settings of 8 data switches
        ADD   HL,BC            ;Add manual offset to start of RAM1
        LD    (HL),A           ;Store manual data value into RAM1
COMPLETE:RET
;
;****************************************************************
;Subroutine PROGRAM
;This programs the EPROM.  This involves transferring 2K bytes
;from RAM1 through PIO2 to the EPROM held in the ZIF socket.
;The CS, PD/PGM and Vpp control signals must be set correctly
;when each byte is programmed.
;                 STRUCTURE
```

```
; BEGIN
;     REPEAT
;           SET EPROM DATA PINS
;           SET EPROM ADDRESS (LOWER) PINS
;           SET EPROM ADDRESS (UPPER) PINS, PD/PGM HIGH
;           DELAY
;           SET EPROM ADDRESS (UPPER) PINS, PD/PGM LOW
;     UNTIL 2K BYTES ARE PROGRAMMED IN EPROM
; END
; System outputs: EPROM data (address 08)
;                 EPROM address - lower (address 09)
;                               - higher (address 09, bits 0,1,2)
;                 EPROM control signals - CS (address 09, bit 0)
;                                       - PD/PGM (address 09, bit 1)
;                                       - Vpp (address 09, bit 2)
;
 PROGRAM: LD   DE, 07FFH      ; Loop count (and end address of EPROM)
          LD   HL, 47FFH      ; End address of RAM1
          LD   B, 38H         ; Bit pattern for Vpp, PD/PGM & CS at 1
    LOOP: LD   A, (HL)        ; Data byte from RAM1
          OUT  (PIO2C), A     ; Set on EPROM data pins
          LD   A, E           ; Lower half of EPROM address
          OUT  (PIO2A), A     ; Set on EPROM address pins
          LD   A, D           ; Upper half of EPROM address
          OR   B              ; Add Vpp, PD/PGM and CS set to 1
          OUT  (PIO2B), A     ; Set on EPROM address (& control) pins
          CALL DELAY          ; Delay for 50 ms (program one byte)
          RES  4, A           ; Reset bit 4 in A (set PD/PGM to 0)
          OUT  (PIO2B), A     ; Set on EPROM address (& control) pins
          DEC  HL             ; Decrement address in RAM1
          DEC  DE             ; Decrement loop count (EPROM address)
          LD   A, E           ; Transfer E to A
          OR   D              ; Comparing A and D
          JP   NZ, LOOP       ; Repeat if not the same
          RET
;
; *****************************************************************
; Subroutine DELAY
; This generates a 50 ms delay (the time to program one byte into
; EPROM).
;               STRUCTURE
; BEGIN
;     SET DELAY COUNT FOR 50MS
;     REPEAT
;           DECREMENT DELAY COUNT
;     UNTIL DELAY COUNT IS ZERO
; END
    DELAY: PUSH BC            ; Preserve BC on stack
           LD   BC, 2500      ; Set delay loop count for 50 ms
    PAUSE: DEC  BC            ; Decrement
           LD   A, B          ; Transfer B to A
           OR   C             ; Are A and C the same (zero)?
```

```
        JP    NZ,PAUSE      ;Repeat if not
        POP   BC            ;Reinstate BC from stack
        RET
; ****************************************************************
        END
```

11.4 Exercises

(1) Write down the two changes you would make to the control program to program 2708 EPROMs in place of 2716 EPROMs (assume that the EPROMs are pin-compatible, except that a 2708 does not possess an A10 pin).

(2) Write down the changes you would make to the control program if the hardware arrangement shown in figure 11.6 is added. The hexadecimal display should change when the operator presses the ENTER push-button and should indicate the setting of the 8 data switches.

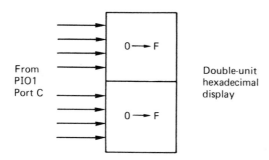

Figure 11.6 Additional hexadecimal display unit

(3) Sketch the additional circuitry, and write down the software changes you would apply (if any), to illuminate a LED when each byte is programmed into the EPROM.

(4) Assume that RAM3 is added to the hardware arrangement at a start address of C000. Write out the program listing for a completely separate program (assume that it is triggered by the NMI interrupt signal, and it is entered at memory location 0066) that reads the contents of the EPROM held in the ZIF socket back into RAM3. Apply the control signal settings shown in figure 11.2.

(5) Although not strictly necessary for this application, write down the changes you would make to the control program to ensure that it responds only once to each operation of the ENTER and PROGRAM

pushbuttons. You could extend this to ignore contact bounce, that is unwanted repeated operation of the ENTER pushbutton on contact closure and contact release – this effect may persist for up to 30 ms.

12 Typical DVM (Digital Voltmeter) Design

12.1 DVM operation

A DVM (Digital Voltmeter) is a multimeter with digital display. It is an ubiquitous item of test equipment that measures voltage, current and resistance. A variety of signal ranges can be selected, and both ac and dc signals can be measured. Some designs are battery-driven and portable, other are mains-driven and desk-mounted. Digital instruments offer the advantage of much higher input impedances compared with their analogue forerunners, for example the 'Avometer', for voltage measurements.

Recent DVM designs are microprocessor-based, and facilities such as auto-ranging can be included. A DVM control circuit is an ideal application for a single-chip microcomputer (sometimes called a 'microcontroller'), so that an 8-bit CPU, memory and input/output ports are contained within a single IC. Sometimes even an A/D converter is built into the IC. The design presented here is more extensive in order to handle a speech synthesiser circuit that 'speaks' the numerical value of the electrical parameter that is being measured. Once again, it is based on a Z80 microprocessor.

12.2 Hardware – circuit diagram

A simplified representation of the circuit diagram is shown in figure 12.1. The signal that is to be measured is shown as 'Analogue signal' – the analogue processing circuit for the different signal types (voltage/current/ resistance) is not shown, for simplicity. It is assumed that the measured voltage range is 0 to +2.55 V.

Four contact-closure signals set by the operator are shown – the three-position switch representing VOLTAGE, CURRENT and RESISTANCE is used to identify the measurement type, and the pushbutton SPEAK is pressed when it is required to hear a new spoken representation of the reading. An eight-digit segment display unit is used to augment the speech synthesiser circuit to indicate the latest reading to the operator. The

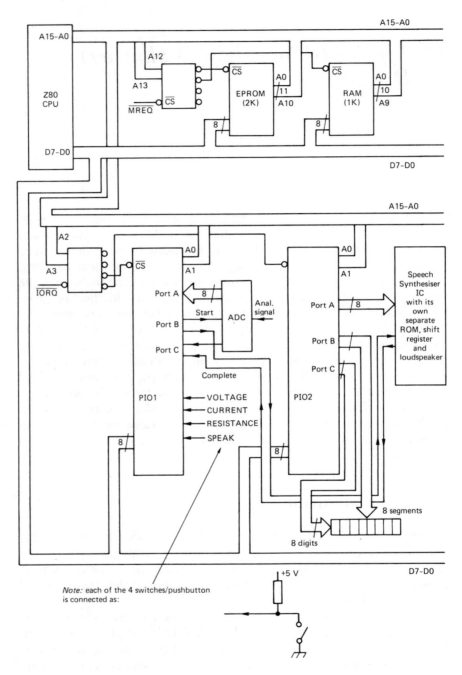

Figure 12.1 Circuit diagram of 'talking' DVM

audio/speech circuit is based on a Speech Synthesiser IC, which is connected to its own ROM or EPROM (containing the bit patterns for each of the 256 spoken words that it can process) and additional shift register (to convert the ROM bytes into a serial pulse stream feeding a loudspeaker). The system of speech generation is as follows:

(a) a byte code is presented to the speech synthesiser, through Port A on PIO2, to select a particular spoken word (1 of 256);
(b) the handshaking bits are set appropriately;
(c) the speech synthesiser IC uses the word code to address a block of locations held in ROM/EPROM;
(d) typically 16 bytes are then presented in turn to a shift register which produces 128 bits (8 bits × 16 bytes) that simulate the word sound on the loudspeaker.

The 8-bit ADC (Analogue-to-Digital Converter) employs a similar handshaking system to that of the Speech Synthesiser IC. The timing diagrams for both pairs of handshaking bits are shown in figure 12.2.

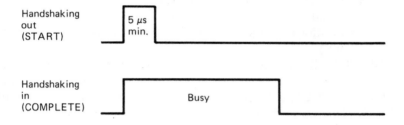

Figure 12.2 Handshaking bits waveforms

The input/output addresses are:

Address	Identity
08	PIO1 port A
09	PIO1 port B
0A	PIO1 port C
0B	PIO1 control register
0C	PIO2 port A
0D	PIO2 port B
0E	PIO2 port C
0F	PIO2 control register

The control program is held in the EPROM, and the RAM is available for its use, for example the stack. Figure 12.3 illustrates the memory map and the way in which the Speech Synthesiser holds its bit streams in its separate look-up ROM (or EPROM). Notice that the vocabulary of the speech synthesiser system is altered by simply changing the stored bit patterns in this look-up ROM/EPROM.

12.3   Software – control program

The modular design of the control program is shown in Figure 12.4. The main program calls six modules (subroutines) as follows:

(a) INIT. This initialises (sets port directions) PIO1 and PIO2.
(b) SPEAKKEY. This polls the SPEAK key until it is pressed by the operator.
(c) ANALIN. This reads the analogue voltage in through the ADC; this involves processing the handshaking bits (START conversion and COMPLETE conversion).
(d) CONVERT. This converts the 8-bit ADC count into three numerical codes destined for the speech synthesiser – these bytes are placed into memory locations 1000 to 1003 (1001 is reserved for the code for the word 'Point').
(e) ADDWORDS. This adds a fourth and fifth byte to the list of three word codes in memory, and represents the setting of the three-position VOLTAGE/CURRENT/RESISTANCE switch and the word 'Point'.
(f) TALK. This sends the five spoken word codes to the Speech Synthesiser IC; this involves handling the handshaking bits.

Note

For simplicity it is assumed that the signal range is fixed, and is spoken in the following sequence:

Digit, 'Point', Digit, Digit, 'Type'

'Type' is 'Volts', 'Amps' or 'Ohms'.

Program listing

```
;Talking DVM program.
;This program reads an input analogue signal, and then 'speaks'
;the numerical value of that signal. The signal can be either
;a voltage, current or resistance, as selected by the operator.
```

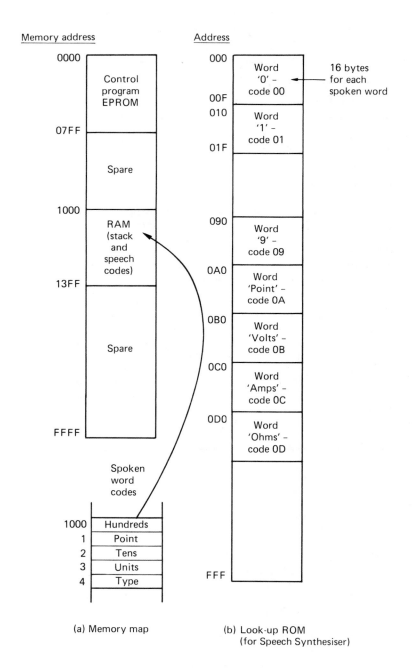

(a) Memory map

(b) Look-up ROM
(for Speech Synthesiser)

Figure 12.3 Memory systems for 'talking' DVM

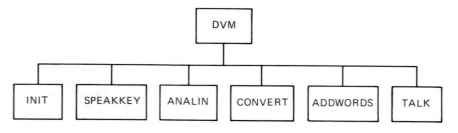

Figure 12.4 Top-down modular design of DVM control program

```
;Main program
            ORG    0000H
    PIO1A EQU    08H            ;8-bit ADC reading
    PIO1B EQU    09H            ;Handshaking bits out
    PIO1C EQU    0AH            ;Handshaking bits in + switch+ p/b
PIO1CONT EQU    0BH            ;Control register for PIO1
    PIO2A EQU    0CH            ;8-bit code to Speech Synthesiser
    PIO2B EQU    0DH            ;8 segment signals to display
    PIO2C EQU    0EH            ;8 digit signals to display
PIO2CONT EQU    0FH            ;Control register for PIO2
            LD     SP,13FFH      ;Set stack pointer at end of RAM
            CALL   INIT          ;Initialise PIOs
      LOOP: CALL   SPEAKKEY      ;Poll SPEAK pushbutton
            CALL   ANALIN        ;Read ADC
            CALL   CONVERT       ;Convert ADC byte to word codes
            CALL   ADDWORDS      ;Add words for 'Point' and Type
            CALL   TALK          ;Speaks words through Speech
                                 Synthesiser
            JP     LOOP          ;Repeat
;
;****************************************************************
;Subroutine INIT
;Initialises the two PIOs
;              STRUCTURE
;BEGIN
;     INITIALISE PIO1
;     INITIALISE PIO2
;END
;System outputs: PIO1 control register (address 0B)
;                PIO2 control register (address 0F)
;
      INIT:LD     A,4DH          ;Control byte for PIO1 port directions
            OUT    (PIO1CONT),A ;Send to control register
            LD     A,40H          ;Control byte for PIO2 port directions
            OUT    (PIO2CONT),A ;Send to control register
            RET
;
;****************************************************************
;Subroutine SPEAKKEY
```

```
;This polls the SPEAK pushbutton until it is pressed.
                STRUCTURE
;BEGIN
;    REPEAT
;          READ SPEAK KEY
;    UNTIL SPEAK KEY IS PRESSED
;END
;System inputs:  SPEAK pushbutton (bit 5, address OA)
;
   SPEAK: IN   A, (PIOC)      ;Poll
          BIT  5, A           ;        the
          JP   NZ, SPEAK      ;              SPEAK pushbutton
          RET
;
;****************************************************************
;Subroutine ANALIN
;This reads in the 8-bit value from the A/D converter.
;This involves generating a START Conversion pulse, waiting
;until COMPLETE Conversion is set and then reading in the
;ADC output.
;                STRUCTURE
;BEGIN
;    GENERATE PULSE ON START SIGNAL
;    REPEAT
;          READ COMPLETE CONVERSION SIGNAL
;    UNTIL COMPLETE IS SET
;    READ IN ADC VALUE
;END
;System inputs:  COMPLETE Conversion (bit 0, address OA)
                  ADC reading (address 08)
;System outputs: START Conversion (bit 0, address 09)
;
   ANALIN: LD   A, 00000001B   ;Set bit 0 to 1
           OUT  (PIO1B), A     ;Set START Conversion to ADC to 1
           NOP                 ;Generate
           NOP                 ;          short delay
           LD   A, 00000000B   ;Set bit 0 to 0
           OUT  (PIO1B), A     ;Set START Conversion to ADC to 0
     WAIT: IN   A, (PIO1C)     ;Wait until
           BIT  0, A           ;          COMPLETE Conversion
           JP   NZ, WAIT       ;                    is set to 0
           IN   A, (PIO1A)     ;Read in ADC count
           RET
;
;****************************************************************
;Subroutine CONVERT
;This converts the ADC reading (0–255) into three counts
;(hundreds, tens, units), and stores in memory locations 1000
;to 1003. These counts are later given to the Speech Synthesiser
;to 'speak' the ADC reading.
;                STRUCTURE
;BEGIN
```

```
;      REPEAT
;            SUBTRACT 100 FROM ADC READING
;            INCREMENT HUNDREDS COUNT
;      UNTIL ADC READING < 100
;      REPEAT
;            SUBTRACT 10 FROM ADC READING (REMAINDER)
;            INCREMENT TENS COUNT
;      UNTIL ADC READING (REMAINDER) < 10
;      STORE HUNDREDS, TENS, UNITS INTO MEMORY
; END
;
  CONVERT: LD    B, O          ; Set hundreds count to 0
           CP    100           ; Jump if ADC
           JP    M, DONEHUN    ;          value below 100
           INC   B             ; Increment hundreds count to 1
           SUB   100           ; Subtract 100 from ADC value
           CP    100           ; Jump if ADC
           JP    M, DONEHUN    ;          value below 100
           INC   B             ; Increment hundreds count to 2
           SUB   100           ; Subtract 100 from ADC value
  DONEHUN: LD    C, O          ; Set tens count to 0
   REPEAT: CP    10            ; Jump if ADC
           JP    M, DONETEN    ;          value below 10
           SUB   10            ; Subtract 10 from ADC value
           INC   C             ; Increment tens count
           JP    REPEAT        ; Repeat
  DONETEN: LD    (1003H), A    ; Store units in 1003
           LD    A, C          ; Store tens
           LD    (1002H), A    ;          in 1002
           LD    A, B          ; Store hundreds
           LD    (1000H), A    ;                in 1000
           RET
;
; ****************************************************************
; Subroutine ADDWORDS
; This adds the spoken words 'Point' and Type ('Volts', Amps'
; or 'Ohms') to the memory list of the three words representing
; the numerical value of the input reading – locations 1000 to
; 1004.
;                 STRUCTURE
; BEGIN
;     STORE WORD CODE FOR 'POINT' IN MEMORY
;     IF VOLTAGE SWITCH IS SET
;          STORE WORD CODE FOR VOLTAGE
;     ELSE IF CURRENT SWITCH IS SET
;          STORE WORD CODE FOR CURRENT
;     ELSE STORE WORD CODE FOR RESISTANCE
; END
; System inputs:  3-position switch (bits 2, 3, and 4, address OA)
;
  VOLTAGE EQU   OBH
  CURRENT EQU   OCH
RESISTAN EQU   ODH
```

```
ADDWORDS: LD    A, OAH          ; Code for spoken word 'Point'
          LD    (1001H), A      ; Add to memory list
          IN    A, (PIO1C)      ; Input 3-position switch
          BIT   2, A            ; Check if
          JP    NZ, NOTVOLTS    ;              Voltage set
          LD    B, VOLTAGE      ; Set word code
          JP    STORE           ;              for voltage
NOTVOLTS: BIT   3, A            ; Check if
          JP    NZ, NOTCURR     ;              Current set
          LD    B, CURRENT      ; Set word code
          JP    STORE           ;              for  current
NOTCURR:  LD    B, RESISTAN     ; Must be Resistance set
STORE:    LD    A, B            ; Store word code
          LD    (1004H), A      ;              into memory
          RET
;
; **************************************************************
; Subroutine TALK
; This sends the list of five spoken words to the Speech
; Synthesiser.  The handshaking bits must be processed correctly
; for each word.
;               STRUCTURE
; BEGIN
;     REPEAT
;          SEND SPOKEN WORD CODE TO SPEECH SYNTHESISER
;          SEND PULSE ON HANDSHAKING SIGNAL 'START'
;          REPEAT
;               READ HANDSHAKING 'COMPLETE' SIGNAL
;          UNTIL COMPLETE IS SET
;     UNTIL FIVE WORDS ARE SPOKEN
; END
; System inputs:   COMPLETE from Speech Synthesiser (bit 1, addr OA)
; System outputs:  START for Speech Synthesiser (bit 1, address 09)
;                  Word code for Speech Synthesiser (address OC)
     TALK: LD    B, 5           ; Loop count for 5 spoken words
           LD    HL, 1000H      ; Start address in memory of 5 words
 SENTENCE: LD    A, (HL)        ; Fetch a spoken word code from memory
           OUT   (PIO2A), A     ; Send to Speech Synthesiser
           LD    A, 00000010B   ; Set bit 1 to 1
           OUT   (PIOB), A      ; Set START to Speech Synthesiser to 1
           NOP                  ; Generate
           NOP                  ;         short delay
           LD    A, 00000000B   ; Set bit 1 to 0
           OUT   (PIO1B), A     ; Set START to Speech Synthesiser to 0
 SPEAKING: IN    A, (PIO1C)     ; Wait until
           BIT   1, A           ;              COMPLETE
           JP    NZ, SPEAKING   ;                   is set to 0
           INC   HL             ; Point to next word in memory
           DEC   B              ; Loop
           JP    NZ, SENTENCE;        5 times
           RET
; **************************************************************
           END
```

12.4   Exercises

(1) The program listing above does not include the module (subroutine) that displays the numerical reading on the 8-digit segment display. Assume that such a subroutine is to be added to the program. Where would you place the CALL instruction so that the display is refreshed continuously (rather than only when the SPEAK pushbutton is pressed)?

(2) Which single IC requires to be changed if the device is to speak in a language other than English?

(3) Write down the additions you would make to the control program if the following message is to be spoken before the numerical reading is given: 'The current reading is'. Assume that these four words possess adjacent word codes 20 to 23 in the Speech Synthesiser vocabulary.

(4) Sketch the additional circuitry that is necessary if it is required to send the numerical reading to a remote computer by RS232-C data link.

13 Typical Bootstrap Loader Design

13.1 Role of bootstrap loader

The 'operating system' is the master program in a disk-based computer, and it is used to activate and control all other programs (or 'files' or 'jobs') in the system. It is invariably held on disk in PCs (Personal Computers), and hence must be transferred to RAM when the computer is switched on. This task is performed by a 'bootstrap loader' program, which is ROM-based and is entered automatically on switch-on (or 'Reset', that is when the RESET pushbutton is pressed).

It is possible to build some hardware test routines into the bootstrap loader, for example RAM read/write test, ROM checksum tests and CRT message display.

13.2 Hardware – circuit diagram

Most PCs are based on the Intel 8088/8086 family of 16-bit micro-processors, which include the 8088, 8086, 80186, 80286 and 80386 (the latter is a 32-bit device). These computers include the IBM PC (including XT and AT versions), Amstrad PC, ACT Sirius, DEC Rainbow, Apricot and others.

A generalised circuit diagram of the microprocessor section of an 8088-based PC is shown in figure 13.1. The bootstrap loader program is held in the EPROM, and is automatically entered on Reset, that is when the computer is switched on or when the RESET pushbutton is pressed. Most PCs possess 256K or 512K of RAM for use by the operating system and the supporting software. However, only 1K of RAM is shown here for use by the operating system as stack. Although the 8088 is a 16-bit microprocessor, its external data bus is only 8-bits wide. Additionally it shares the same pins on the CPU as the lower 8 address lines (A7–A0), and hence it must be de-multiplexed to create the separate data and address bus signals before feeding the memory circuit.

The memory map is shown in figure 13.2. The Intel 8088/8086 CPUs possess internal 16-bit addressing registers (Code Segment, Data Segment,

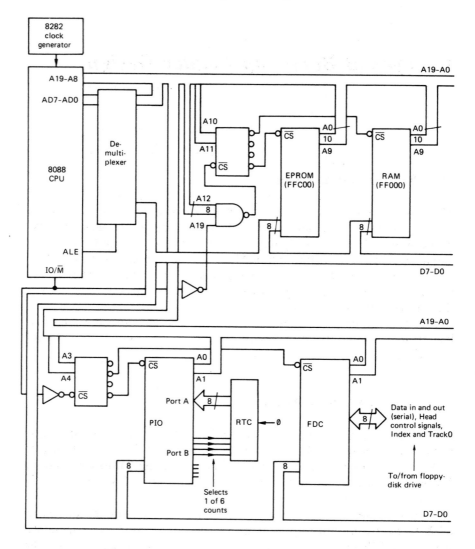

Figure 13.1 Circuit diagram of central section of personal computer

Stack Segment) that are selectively added to each memory address used in the program, and the method the CPU applies to compute the start addresses of RAM (stack) and EPROM (program) is shown on the right-hand side of the diagram – the reader is referred to the Bibliography at the end of the chapter for a full description of the memory segmentation features of the Intel devices. Notice that the Reset address for the 8088/8086 is FFFF0 (Code Segment Register is set to FFFF and Program

Memory address

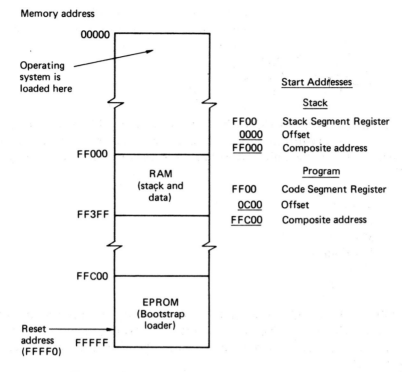

Figure 13.2 Memory map for 8088-based PC

Counter is set to 0000 on Reset), and therefore the EPROM containing the Bootstrap Loader must contain this address.

Bytes are transferred on and off disk through the Floppy-Disk Controller (FDC) IC. Data are transferred in serial form via the Read/Write windings to the rotating disk, and four head control signals (Head Step, Head Direction, Head Read/Write, Head Load) are used. Additionally, two position feedback signals (Index and Track 0) are applied to enable the FDC to initialise its track and sector counters. The four addresses on the FDC are shown in the following table of input/output addresses:

Address	Identity
08	FDC data register
09	FDC track register
0A	FDC sector register
0B	FDC command/status register (bit 0 is set to 1 when head is over required track and sector,

bit 1 is set to 1 when byte has been
transferred – set to 0 during byte transfer)

18	PIO port A
19	PIO port B
1A	Not used
1B	PIO control register

The Real-Time Clock (RTC) IC is connected to the PIO ports, and it is a separately battery-driven device that operates even when the computer is switched off. It maintains six counts, representing the time-of-day, as follows:

Seconds
10 seconds
Minutes
10 minutes
Hours
10 hours

PIO port B is used to select/address each count, which is read in to the CPU through port A. The purpose of the RTC is to enable the operating system to keep track of real-time, which can be displayed to the operator on the CRT.

13.3   Software

A much simplified representation of the bootstrap loader program is presented here. Its purpose is to illustrate the software control over such useful interfacing devices as the FDC and RTC. Notes at the end of this section describe some of the extended facilities provided in a proprietary bootstrap loader.

Figure 13.3 illustrates the modular form of the program. The functions of the modules are:

(a) INIT. This initialises (sets port directions) the PIO.
(a) DISKREAD. This transfers the operating system from disk (track 0, sectors 1 to 64) to memory (start address 00000) through the FDC.
(c) CLOCK. This reads the current time in from the RTC and places the time counts into six consecutive memory locations.
(d) HEADOK. This waits until a disk head movement has been completed.
(e) DISKBUSY. This waits until a byte has been transferred off disk.

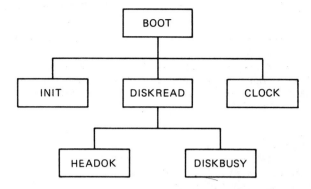

Figure 13.3 Top-down modular design of bootstrap loader program

Program listing

```
;Bootstrap loader program (simplified).
;This program transfers the operating system from floppy disk
;into memory, and then enters the operating system. The
;time-of-day is read from a Real-Time Clock device. Written in
;8088 mnemonics.
;Main program
          CODE  SEGMENT
          ORG   0000H
          ASSUME CS:0FFC0H
          MOV   AX,0FF00H    ;Load Stack Segment
          MOV   SS,AX        ;                with FF00
          MOV   AX,03FFH     ;Load Stack Pointer
          MOV   SP,AX        ;                with 03FF
          MOV   AX,0000H     ;Load Data Segment
          MOV   DS,AX        ;                with 0000
          CALL  INIT         ;Initialise PIO
          CALL  DISKREAD     ;Read operating system from disk
          CALL  CLOCK        ;Read Real-Time Clock
          JMP   OPERSYS      ;Enter operating system
;
;****************************************************************
;Subroutine INIT
;Initialises the PIO
;               STRUCTURE
;BEGIN
;     INITIALISE PIO
;END
;System outputs: PIO control register (address 1B)
;
 PIOCONT EQU  1BH
    INIT:MOV  AL,06H         ;Control byte for PIO port directions
         OUT  PIOCONT,AL     ;Send to control register
```

```
                RET
;
; ****************************************************************
; Subroutine DISKREAD
; Transfers the 8K operating system from (track 0, sectors
; 1 to 64) into memory (start address 0000). Internal loop
; transfers 128 bytes; outer loop transfers 64 sectors.
;                    STRUCTURE
; BEGIN
;     REPEAT
;           REPEAT
;                 TRANSFER 1 BYTE FROM DISK
;           UNTIL 128 BYTES ARE TRANSFERRED
;     UNTIL 64 SECTORS ARE TRANSFERRED
; END
; System inputs:   FDC data register (address 08)
; System outputs:  FDC track register (address 09)
;                  FDC sector register (address 0A)
;
     DATA   EQU  08H
     TRACK  EQU  09H
     SECTOR EQU  0AH
DISKREAD: MOV   BX, 0000H    ; Base address for operating system
          MOV   AL, 00H      ; Track 0
          OUT   TRACK, AL    ; Output to track register
          MOV   CL, 64       ; 64 sectors (8K) to be transferred
          MOV   CH, 1        ; Initialise sector count
 SECTORS: MOV   AL, CH       ; Sector count
          OUT   SECTOR. AL   ; Output to sector register
          CALL  HEADOK       ; Wait until head has settled
          MOV   DL, 128      ; 128 bytes per sector
          MOV   DH, 0        ; Byte count
   BYTES: CALL  DISKBUSY     ; Wait until byte is transferred
          IN    AL, DATA     ; Input data byte from disk
          MOV   (BX), AL     ; Store into RAM
          INX   BX           ; Increment RAM address
          INC   DH           ; Increment byte count
          DEC   DL           ; Repeat for
          JNZ   BYTES        ;             128 bytes (1 sector)
          INC   CH           ; Increment sector counter
          DEC   CL           ; Repeat for
          JNZ   SECTORS      ;             64 sectors (8K)
          RET
;
; ****************************************************************
; Subroutine CLOCK
; Reads six time-of-day counts from Real-Time Clock into memory
; locations FFFA to FFFE.
;                    STRUCTURE
; BEGIN
;     REPEAT
;           OUTPUT ADDRESS  OF COUNT IN RTC
```

```
;              INPUT COUNT FROM RTC
;              STORE COUNT IN MEMORY
;       UNTIL SIX COUNTS ARE READ
; END
; System inputs:   RTC count, PIO port A (address 18)
; System outputs:  RTC address, PIO port B (bits 0, 1, 2, address 19)
;
      PIOA  EQU   18H
      PIOB  EQU   19H
      CLOCK: MOV  BX, 0FFFAH     ; Memory start address for RTC counts
             MOV  CL, 6          ; Loop count for 6 counts
             MOV  CH, 0          ; Initialise RTC count address
   RTCREAD: MOV  AL, CH          ; Output
             OUT  PIOB, AL       ;          RTC count address
             IN   AL, PIOA       ; Input RTC count
             MOV  (BX), AL        ; Store in memory
             INC  BX             ; Increment memory address
             INC  CH             ; Increment RTC count address
             DEC  CL             ; Repeat
             JNZ  RTCREAD        ;          for 6 counts
             RET
; ********************************************************************
; Subroutine HEADOK
; Waits until disk head movement (to required track and sector)
; is completed.
;                   STRUCTURE
; BEGIN
;      REPEAT
;             READ FDC HEAD STATIONARY BIT
;      UNTIL HEAD IS STATIONARY
; END
; System inputs:   HEAD busy bit (bit 0, address 0B)
;
COMMSTAT EQU   0BH
   HEADOK: IN    AL, COMMSTAT   ; Read FDC command/status register
           AND   AL, 01H        ; Remove all bits except bit 0
           JZE   HEADOK         ; Poll Head Stationary bit
           RET
;
; ********************************************************************
; Subroutine DISKBUSY
; Waits until FDC has completed the transfer (serial form) of
; one byte.
;                   STRUCTURE
; BEGIN
;      REPEAT
;             READ FDC TRANSFER COMPLETE BIT
;      UNTIL TRANSFER IS COMPLETE
; END
;
COMMSTAT EQU   0BH
DISKBUSY: IN    AL, COMMSTAT   ; Read FDC command/status register
```

```
        AND   AL, 02      ;Remove all bits except bit 1
        JZE   DISKBUSY    ;Poll Transfer Complete bit
        RET
; ****************************************************************
        END
```

Note

In this simplified program, several factors were omitted:

(1) The 'Read/Write' bit in the FDC command/status register was not used. Clearly data can be transferred in both directions, although this feature was not illustrated in this example.
(2) In most DOS systems (PC-DOS and MS-DOS), the bootstrap loader is itself disk-based (track 0, sector 1). On Reset, a ROM-based 'Executive' program is entered automatically, and this loads the bootstrap loader from disk into memory (the last 8K of the first 64K block).
(3) It is possible for the bootstrap loader to perform some automatic hardware tests, for example RAM cycle, ROM checksum, as well as clearing video RAM.
(4) No CRT display messages are presented to guide the operator, for example to indicate disk transfer failure.
(5) Typical FDCs can control more than one floppy disk drive, and several additional bits in the command/status register would have to be processed.
(6) Most floppy disk systems are not able to store a full 8K on a single track – typically a sector may be 256 bytes, and 15 sectors can be stored on a track.

13.4   Exercises

(1) What instruction must be loaded at memory address FFFF0 (the RESET address)?
(2) Redraw the top-down modular drawing of the program to include RAM test and ROM test procedures.
(3) Assume that bit 2 in the FDC command/status register is set to 1 when the floppy disk is write-protected. Write down the program extensions to detect this condition and to write a marker flag of FF into memory location FFF0 when it ocurs.
(4) What changes to the circuit diagram are necessary if the 1K RAM is to have a start address of FF400?

Bibliography

1. R. C. Holland, *Microprocessors and their Operating Systems,* Pergamon, 1989.
2. R. McMullan, *MS/PC-DOS Prompt,* 1986.
3. C. Jackson, *MS-DOS and PC-DOS on the IBM PC,* Glentop, 1986.

Appendix A: Microprocessor Data Sheets

Intel 8085
Zilog Z80
MOS Technology 6502
Motorola 6809
Microcontrollers (Single-chip Microcomputers)
Intel 8086 (& 80186 & 80286)
Zilog Z8000
Motorola 68000
32-bit Microprocessors
Inmos Transputer

Intel 8085

Followed on from the 8080, which was a two-chip equivalent of the 8085. Not used in any home computers, but was extremely popular in early (late 1970s) industrial control systems.

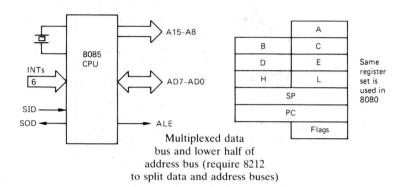

Multiplexed data
bus and lower half of
address bus (require 8212
to split data and address buses)

Start addresses of Interrupt	*PIOs*
Service Routines:	8155 – 3 ports, 256 bytes RAM
RESET – 0000	8255 – 3 ports
TRAP – 0024	8355 – 2 ports, 2K ROM
RST5.5 – 002C	8755 – 2 ports, 2K EPROM
RST6.5 – 0034	
RST7.5 – 003C	
INTR – from interrupting device	

Other 8251 – USART	8202 – Dynamic RAM controller
support 8253 – CTC (3 counters)	8257 – DMA controller
devices: 8271 – FDC	8257 – CRT controller

Intel DMA Control System

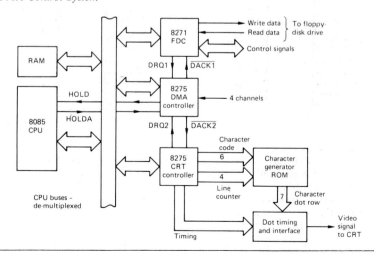

Zilog Z80

Probably the most popular 8-bit microprocessor. Used in home computers (Spectrum, Amstrad, Tandy), office computers and industrial controllers.

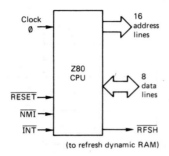

A	F	A′	F′
B	C	B′	C′
D	E	D′	E′
H	L	H′	L′
Interrupt vector I	Memory refresh R		
Index register IX			
Index register IY			
Stack pointer			

Based on the Intel 8085, but possesses second set of registers.

ISR (Interrupt Service Routine) start addresses

RESET – 0000
  NMI – 0066
  INT – CPU obeys contents of Interrupt Vector for CPU 'mode 0'
    – 0038 for CPU 'mode 1'
    – XXYY for CPU 'mode 2' (XX is contents of Interrupt Vector
               YY is supplied on Data Bus from interrupting device)
  'Vector' (CPU examines XXYY to find start address of ISR)

Z80 PIO

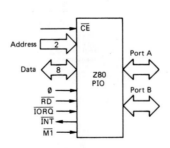

4 addresses:
  00 – Port A (data)
  01 – Port A (control)
  10 – Port B (data)
  11 – Port B (control)
Send 0F to Control register for output port, 4F for input port.

Z80 CTC

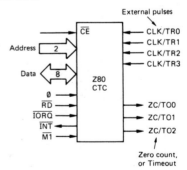

4 channels (counters). Each possesses its own control register – same address as counter.

Zilog Z80

Z80 DART

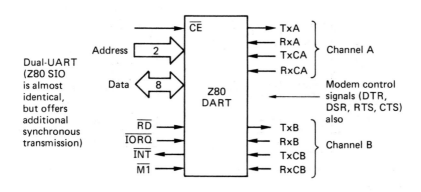

Dual-UART
(Z80 SIO
is almost
identical,
but offers
additional
synchronous
transmission)

Z80 'Daisy-chain' Interrupt System

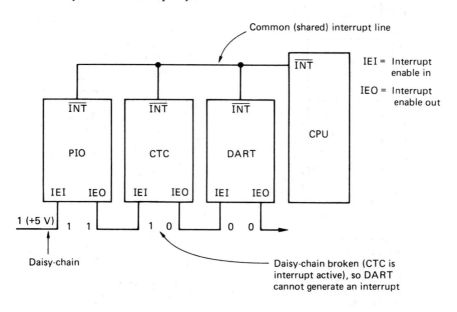

IEI = Interrupt enable in

IEO = Interrupt enable out

Daisy-chain broken (CTC is interrupt active), so DART cannot generate an interrupt

MOS Technology 6502

Very popular 8-bit microprocessor used in home computers, such as BBC, Apple 2, Acorn Atom, Commodore PET and VIC 20.

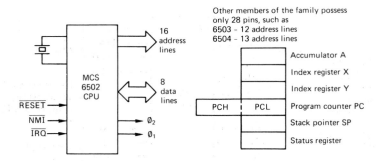

Memory Map

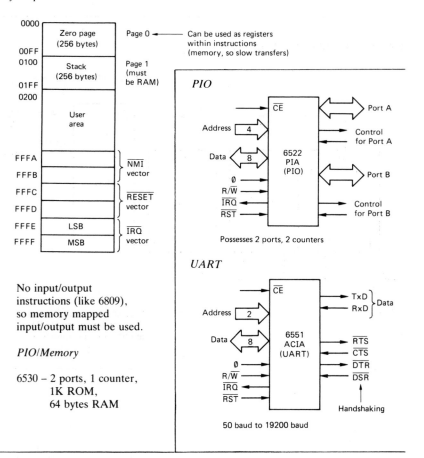

Motorola 6809

Developed by Motorola when
the 6502's popularity
exceeded that of Motorola's
6800. Probably the most
powerful 8-bit
microprocessor (possesses
multiply and divide
instructions and some
16-bit operations).

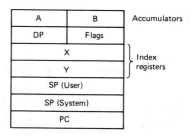

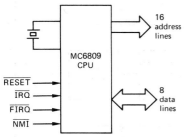

A and B can be combined as
a 16-bit register D.

Predecessor 6800 does not
possess DP (Direct Page),
Y or second SP.

Memory Map

PIO

UART

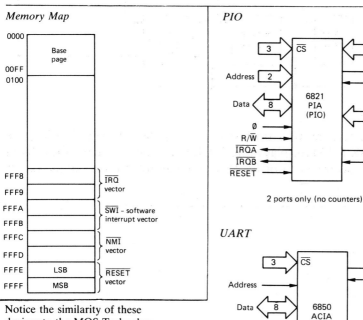

2 ports only (no counters)

Notice the similarity of these
devices to the MOS Technology
support devices (6522 PIO
and 6551 UART). These devices
can be used with the 6809.

Also

6839 – mathematics firmware
6829 – memory management unit

Motorola 6809

Application – VDU Design

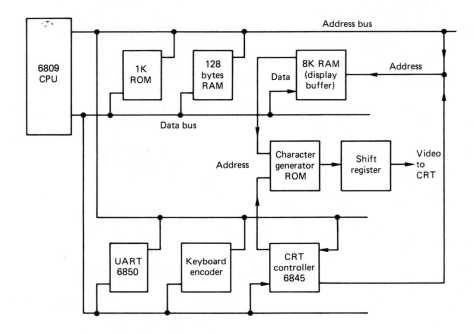

ASCII characters received from remote computer (through UART) are loaded into 8K RAM (display buffer). CRT controller removes these bytes and uses Character generator ROM to generate row for the dot matrix for each character.

Microcontrollers (Single-chip Microcomputers)

These devices employ 8-bit CPUs, but include some memory and input/output. This single-chip solution often produces a smaller and cheaper assembly for such applications as:

(a) washing machine controller;
(b) telephone answering machine.

The instruction set is not normally easy to use, and instructions are 1 or 2 bytes long.

Typical pin functions:

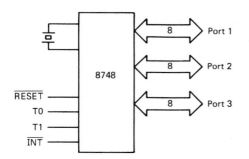

Sometimes the address
and data bus lines
are multiplexed with
the port lines to
allow external
devices to be connected.

Intel Microcontrollers

The most commonly used members of the Intel family are:

(1) 8048 – 3 ports, 1 counter, 64 bytes RAM, 1K ROM
(2) 8748 – 3 ports, 1 counter, 64 bytes RAM, 1K EPROM
(3) 8035 – 3 ports, 1 counter, 64 bytes RAM (no ROM)
(4) 8049 – 3 ports, 1 counter, 128 bytes RAM, 2K ROM
(5) 8022 – 3 ports, 1 counter, 64 bytes RAM, 1K ROM, 1 ADC
(6) 8051 – 3 ports, 1 counter, 128 bytes RAM, 4K ROM, 1 UART plus
       extra instructions (for example, multiply and divide)

Zilog Microcontrollers

(1) Z8601 – 4 ports, 2 counters, 1 UART, 144 bytes RAM, 2K ROM
(2) Z8602 – 4 ports, 2 counters, 1 UART, memory buses
(3) Z8603 – 4 ports, 2 counters, 1 UART, 144 bytes RAM, 2K ROM,
       2K EPROM ('piggy-backed' on top of device)
(4) Z8681 – 4 ports, 2 counters, 1 UART, memory buses
(5) Z8611, Z8612 and Z8613 – 4K versions of (1), (2) and (3)
(6) Z8671 – as (1) with BASIC interpreter

Intel 8086 (& 80186 & 80286)

This is the most popular 16-bit microprocessor family and is based on the 8086/8088 devices. One of the derivatives (8088, 80186 or 80286) is used in nearly all DOS-based 16-bit office computers (IBM PC, Amstrad, Apricot, Sirius). Intel were the first manufacturer to produce 16-bit devices and took control of the market.

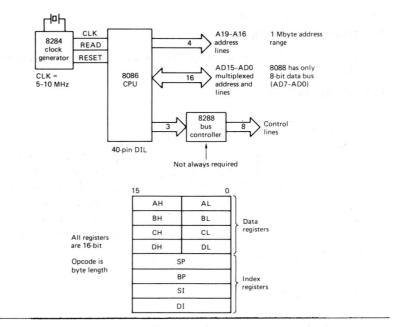

CPU Architecture (of 8086 & 8088)

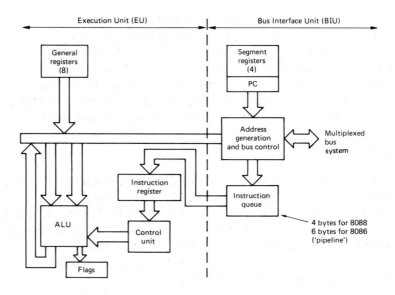

Intel 8086 (& 80186 & 80286)

Instructions are pre-fetched from memory and placed in Instruction Queue (or 'pipeline') to increase program execution speeds. The segment registers allow program (code), data and stack to occupy different 64K memory segments.

Memory Segmentation

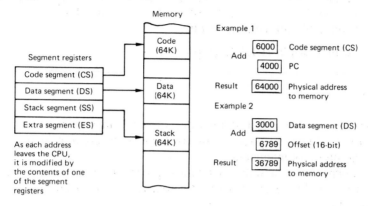

Application of 8086 (Apricot Computer)

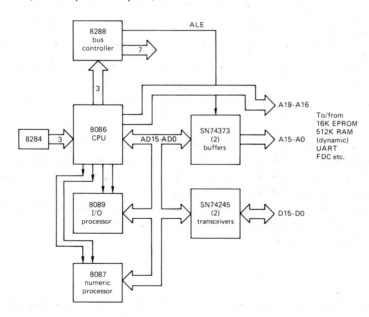

1. The 8087 performs floating point arithmetic (+ high precision fixed point arithmetic, mathematical functions, such as SINE).
2. The 8089 handles I/O transfers (such as DMA transfers to/from floppy or hard disk).

Intel 8086 (& 80186 & 80286)

80186

As 8086, plus the following on-chip functions:
1. Clock generator   2. Chip select logic (7 I/O, 6 memory)
3. Timers (3)   4. DMA control (2 channels)
5. Programmable interrupt controller.

Mounted in a 64-pin JEDEC 'chip carrier'.

80286

Similar to the 8086, but it provides memory management and virtual memory facilities. Segment registers have a different role in order to perform 'memory management':
Program change occurs, and segment registers point to memory locations, from which 48-bit segment descriptor registers are transferred to a 'cache' on the CPU.

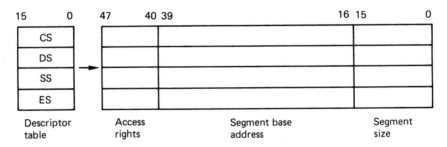

Program is then implemented using these 48-bit registers to provide physical memory addressing (with 'access rights', such as write protect).

Additionally, 'virtual memory' (disk is treated as an extension of memory), allows a file to be transferred from disk although its address is specified as if it is in memory – descriptor table indicates that file is not in memory, interrupt is generated, operating system initiates a DMA transfer to load file into memory.

Note

The 80286 is used in the IBM PC 'AT' version (AT = Advanced Technology). It can be supported by its own Numeric Co-processor (the 80287) to perform hardware floating point arithmetic. Additionally the 80130 OSP (Operating System Firmware Procedssor) can act as a co-processor to the 8086 or 8088 in order to extend the instruction set.

Zilog Z8000

The Zilog 16-bit family has not achieved the popularity of the Intel 8086, or even the Motorola 68000, families, which is a shame because the Zilog devices offer a powerful range of facilities. There are four members of the family:

(a) Z8001 – 23 address lines, 16 data lines (48-pin DIL package);
(b) Z8002 – 16 address lines, 16 data lines (40-pin DIL package);
(c) Z8003 and
(d) Z8004 – both similar to the Z8001 but offering virtual memory.

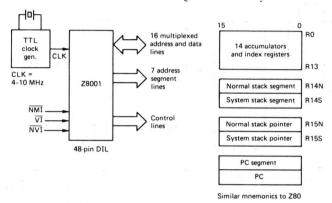

CPU operates in 'System' or 'Normal' modes, for example, can only perform I/O instructions when in System mode.

Z80 Memory Management Unit

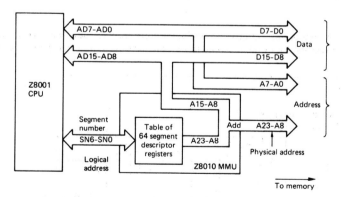

The segment number (effectively the top 7 of the 23 address lines) is used in the MMU to generate a 16-bit block identifier. This allows the operating system to relocate a program anywhere in physical memory. Also access rights (such as read-only, no DMA) can be set.

Support Devices

Z8030 – Serial Communications Controller (double-UART)
Z8031 – Double-UART   Z8036 – PIO (2 ports) & CTC (3 channels)
Z8016 – DMA controller   Z8070 – Floating Point Unit
Z8090 – Universal Peripheral Controller (2 1/2 ports, 2 counters)

Motorola 68000

Very powerful 16-bit processor, with 32-bit registers. Easy to use, program and interface. There are four family members:

(a) MC68000 – 24 address lines, 16 data lines (used in Apple Macintosh);
(b) MC68008 – 20 address lnes, 8 data lines (used in Sinclair QL);
(c) MC68010 – as MC68000, with 'virtual memory';
(d) MC68200 – single-chip 68000 (with ROM, RAM, UART, timers).

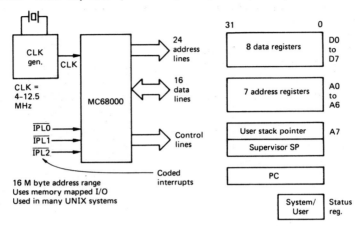

A status flag indicates if the CPU is in 'System' or 'User' mode. In System mode, certain privileged instructions can be used. Only 56 basic mnemonics in the instruction set. A 16-bit opcode with 3 bits specifying register number. 14 addressing modes.

Interrupts

Possesses 256 'exceptions' (interrupts), including software interrupts. First 1K of memory contains 256 vectors, for example, contents of 4 memory locations (bytes) are placed in PC on interrupt.

Application

Using 8-bit support devices:

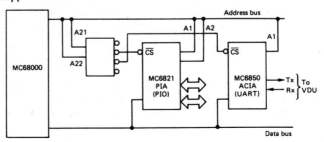

Support Devices

MC68451 – Memory Manager   MC68450 – DMA Controller

32-bit Microprocessors

Advantages over 16-bit devices: (1 gigabyte = 1000M bytes)

(1) 32-bit data manipulation (integer range -2^{31} to $+2^{31}$ -1);
(2) larger memory addressing range (2^{32} = 4 gigabytes);
(3) faster operation (clock speeds 16 MHz to 25 MHz) – typically 2/3 times faster than 16-bit CPUs;
(4) extra instructions and addressing modes;
(5) built-in memory management (convert logical address to physical address, and provide memory protection);
(6) instruction/data cache (on-chip memory holding most frequently addressed instructions and data items).

NMOS or CMOS devices in 84- to 114-pin chip carrier packages. Machine code compatible with their 16-bit predecessors.

Intel 80386 (or '386')

On-chip memory management.
No on-chip instruction/data cache
- typically add 16K static RAM.
Can use the 80287 or 80387
floating point co-processor.

```
        31                      0
        |        | AX   | EAX
        |        | BX   | EBX
        |        | CX   | ECX
        |        | DX   | EDX
        |        | SI   | EDI     Work
        |        | DI   | ESI     registers
        |        | BP   | EBP
        |        | SP   | ESP

                 | CS   |
                 | SS   |
                 | DS   |         Segment
                 | ES   |         registers
                 | FS   |
```

Typical System

80386 CPU
80387 Numeric Co-processor
   16K static RAM memory cache
   4M dynamic RAM main memory
82258 DMA 8272 FDC
82062 Fixed Disk Control
8259A Interrupt Controller
82786 Graphics Co-Processor
82530 Serial Control
82586 LAN (Local Area Network) Control

Zilog Z80000

On-chip memory management.
On-chip cache (16 16-byte entries).
Possesses 6-stage instruction pipeline.
4/5 MIPS (Million Instructions Per
          Second).
System/Normal modes (set by status bit).

```
31                              0
|      30 32-bit work           |
|          registers            |

|      Translation Table        |
|    Descriptor Registers       |
|    (4) – used by Memory        |
|      Management Unit          |
```

EPU (Extended Processing Unit)
The following co-processors:

Z8070 Floating Point Processor
Z8016   DMA   Controller

Normally uses 'Z-bus' backplane.

32-bit Microprocessors

Motorola MC68020

External memory management chip
   (MC68851).
On-chip cache (64 64-bit entries)
   – low 'hit rate', so often use
   additional external cache memory.
Uses memory mapped I/O.
Supervisor/User modes (set by
   status bit).
Powerful 'exception' (interrupt)
   system – 1K byte vector table
(256 4-byte vectors).
MC68881 Floating Point Processor.

> Same register set as
> for 16-bit MC68000,
> in which registers
> are 32-bit.
> Some additional
> registers exist for
> cache control.

Uses 'Versabus' or 'VME' bus backplane.

Inmos Transputer

The transputer (the name is an amalgam of 'transistor' and 'computer') is an example of a RISC (Reduced Instruction Set Computer). It possesses a small instruction set and single-cycle operation, and therefore it is extremely fast in operation (10 MIPS). Several transputers are arranged in arrays to achieve parallel processing or 'concurrency'.

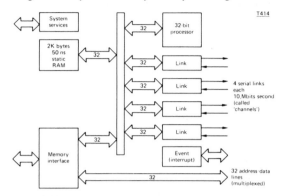

Programmed in a high-level language, 'occam'.

CPUs

(1) T414 – 32-bit, 4 serial links, 2K RAM (see above).
(2) T424 – 32-bit, 4 serial links, 4K RAM.
(3) T212 – 16-bit, 4 serial links, 2K RAM.
(4) T800 – 32-bit, 4 serial links, on-chip floating point proc.

Supporting Devices

(1) F424 floating point transputer.
(2) G412 graphics controller transputer.
(3) M212 disk controller transputer.
(4) C001 and C002 link adaptors (to produce 8-bit parallel link).

Transputer Arrays

Large transputer arrays can rival mainframe computers in processing power. In fact, ICL use a transputer array for the CPU function in their latest machines.

A typical 64 (8 × 8) array, in which the program is distributed throughout the transputers in order to accelerate its execution.

Program sections transfer data via the serial links.

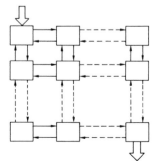

Appendix B: Pin Functions of TTL Digital Integrated Circuits

The serial number of each integrated circuit is

SN74XY

where XY is the two- or three-digit number listed for each device.

There are several families of these TTL (Transistor Transistor Logic) devices, and the most common is the

SN74LS00

family. 'LS' stands for 'Low-power Schottky'.

The material presented in this Appendix is copyright RS Components Limited, Corby, Northants, and reproduced with permission.

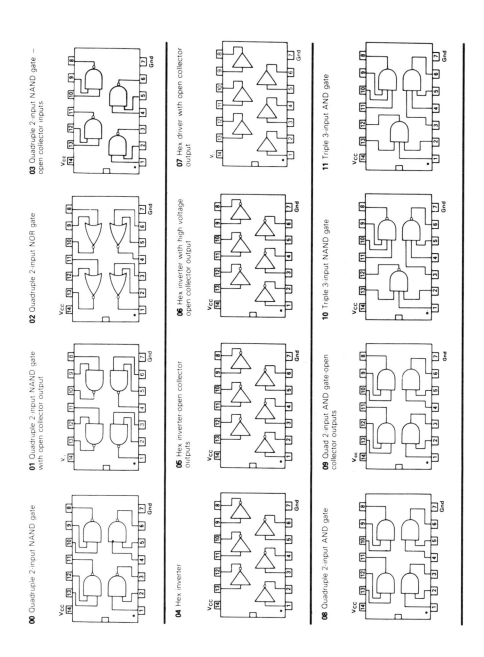

00 Quadruple 2-input NAND gate

01 Quadruple 2-input NAND gate with open collector output

02 Quadruple 2-input NOR gate

03 Quadruple 2-input NAND gate – open collector inputs

04 Hex inverter

05 Hex inverter-open collector outputs

06 Hex inverter with high voltage open collector output

07 Hex driver with open collector output

08 Quadruple 2-input AND gate

09 Quad 2-input AND gate-open collector outputs

10 Triple 3-input NAND gate

11 Triple 3-input AND gate

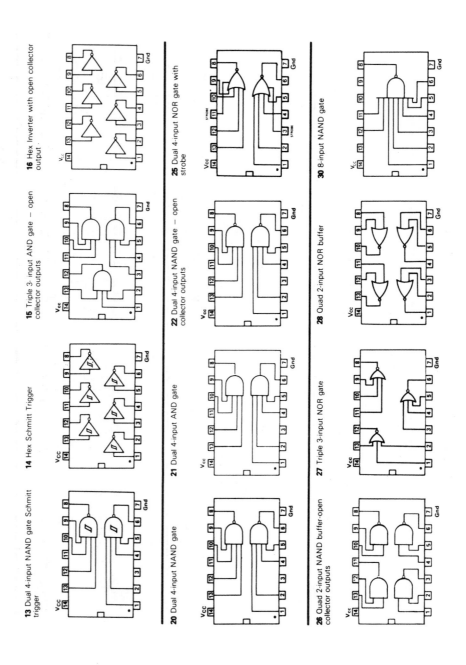

13 Dual 4-input NAND gate Schmitt trigger

14 Hex Schmitt Trigger

15 Triple 3-input AND gate – open collector outputs

16 Hex Inverter with open collector output

20 Dual 4-input NAND gate

21 Dual 4-input AND gate

22 Dual 4-input NAND gate – open collector outputs

25 Dual 4-input NOR gate with strobe

26 Quad 2-input NAND buffer-open collector outputs

27 Triple 3-input NOR gate

28 Quad 2-input NOR buffer

30 8-input NAND gate

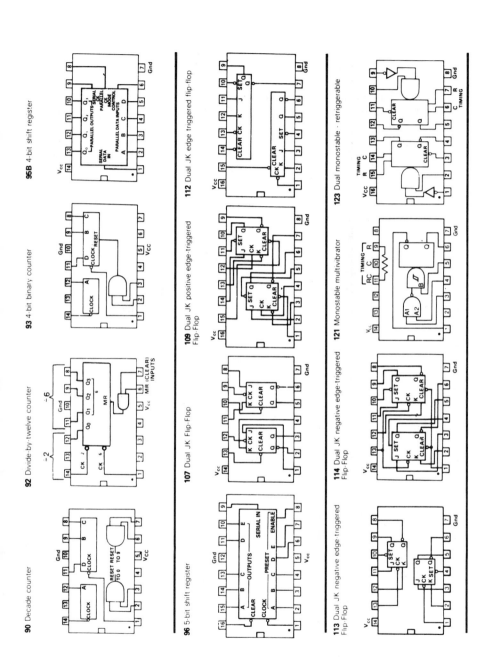

95B 4-bit shift register

93 4-bit binary counter

92 Divide-by-twelve counter

90 Decade counter

112 Dual JK edge triggered flip-flop

109 Dual JK positive edge-triggered Flip Flop

107 Dual JK Flip-Flop

96 5-bit shift register

123 Dual monostable - retriggerable

121 Monostable multivibrator

114 Dual JK negative edge-triggered Flip-Flop

113 Dual JK negative edge-triggered Flip-Flop

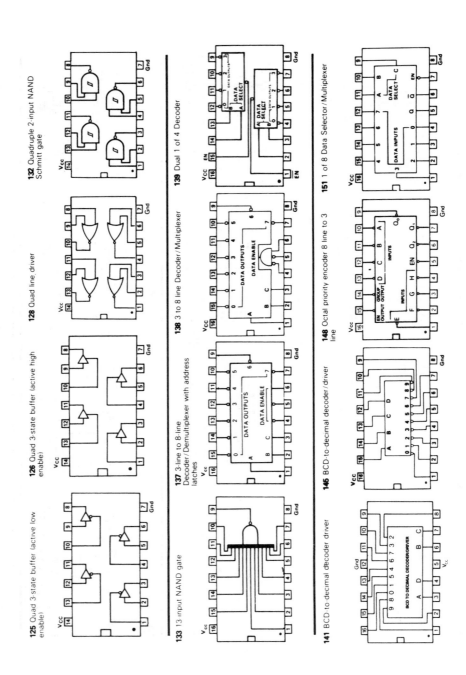

125 Quad 3-state buffer (active low enable)

126 Quad 3-state buffer (active high enable)

128 Quad line driver

132 Quadruple 2-input NAND Schmitt gate

133 13 input NAND gate

137 3-line to 8-line Decoder/Demultiplexer with address latches

138 3 to 8 line Decoder/Multiplexer

139 Dual 1 of 4 Decoder

141 BCD-to-decimal decoder driver

145 BCD-to-decimal decoder/driver

148 Octal priority encoder 8 line to 3 line

151 1 of 8 Data Selector/Multiplexer

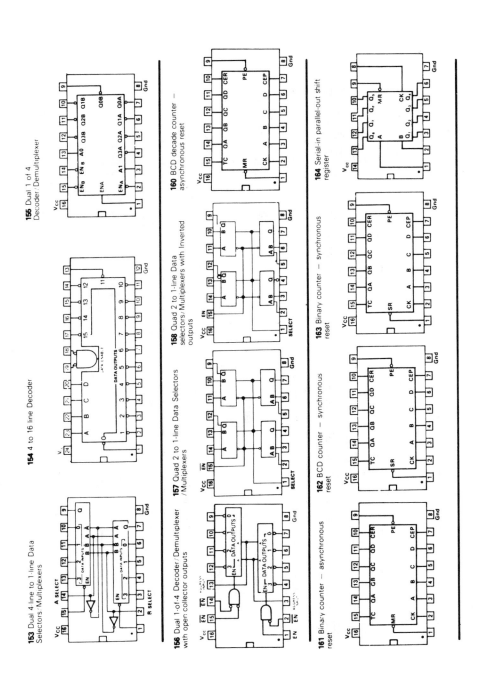

153 Dual 4 line to 1-line Data Selectors/Multiplexers

154 4 to 16 line Decoder

155 Dual 1 of 4 Decoder/Demultiplexer

156 Dual 1-of-4 Decoder/Demultiplexer with open collector outputs

157 Quad 2 to 1-line Data Selectors/Multiplexers

158 Quad 2 to 1-line Data selectors/Multiplexers with Inverted outputs

160 BCD decade counter — asynchronous reset

161 Binary counter — asynchronous reset

162 BCD counter — synchronous reset

163 Binary counter — synchronous reset

164 Serial-in parallel-out shift register

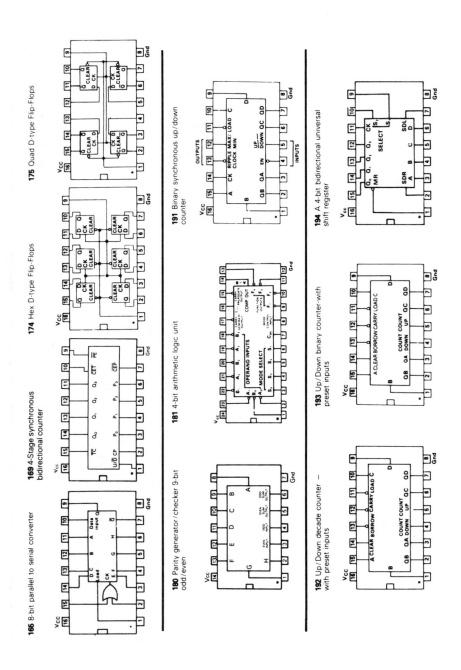

175 Quad D-type Flip-Flops

174 Hex D-type Flip-Flops

169 4-Stage synchronous bidirectional counter

181 4-bit arithmetic logic unit

191 Binary synchronous up/down counter

194 A 4-bit bidirectional universal shift register

165 8-bit parallel to serial converter

180 Parity generator/checker 9-bit odd/even

193 Up/Down binary counter-with preset inputs

192 Up/Down decade counter – with preset inputs

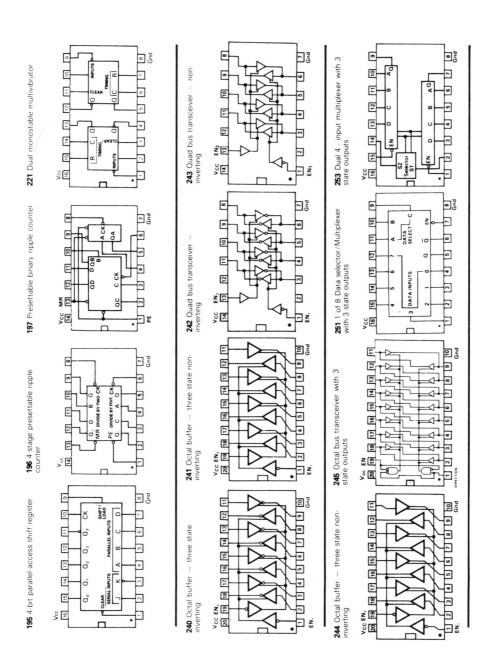

195 4-bit parallel-access shift register

196 4-stage presettable ripple counter

197 Presettable binary ripple counter

221 Dual monostable multivibrator

240 Octal buffer – three state inverting

241 Octal buffer – three state non-inverting

242 Quad bus transceiver – inverting

243 Quad bus transceiver – non-inverting

244 Octal buffer – three state non-inverting

245 Octal bus transceiver with 3 state outputs

251 1 of 8 Data selector/Multiplexer with 3 state outputs

253 Dual 4 - input multiplexer with 3 state outputs

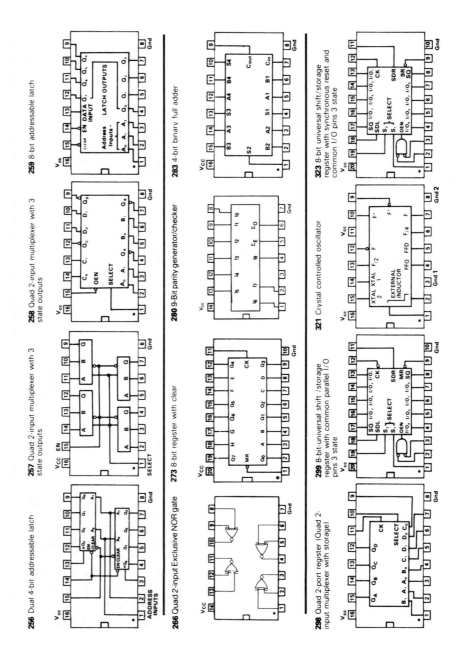

256 Dual 4-bit addressable latch

257 Quad 2-input multiplexer with 3 state outputs

258 Quad 2-input multiplexer with 3 state outputs

259 8-bit addressable latch

266 Quad 2-input Exclusive NOR gate

273 8-bit register with clear

280 9-Bit parity generator/checker

283 4-bit binary full adder

298 Quad 2-port register (Quad 2-input multiplexer with storage)

299 8-bit-universal shift /storage register with common parallel I/O pins 3 state

321 Crystal controlled oscillator

323 8-bit universal shift /storage register with synchronous reset and common I/O pins 3 state

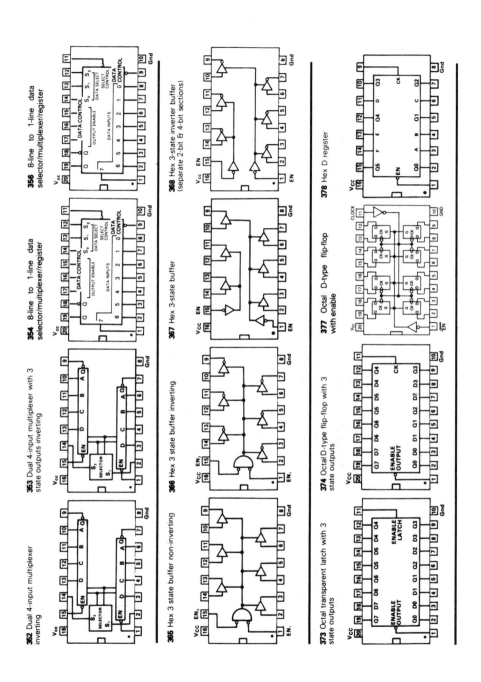

356 8-line to 1-line data selector/multiplexer/register

354 8-line to 1-line data selector/multiplexer/register

363 Dual 4-input multiplexer with 3 state outputs inverting

362 Dual 4-input multiplexer inverting

368 Hex 3-state inverter buffer (separate 2-bit & 4-bit sections)

367 Hex 3-state buffer

366 Hex 3 state buffer inverting

365 Hex 3 state buffer non-inverting

378 Hex D register

377 Octal D-type flip-flop with enable

374 Octal D-type flip-flop with 3 state outputs

373 Octal transparent latch with 3 state outputs

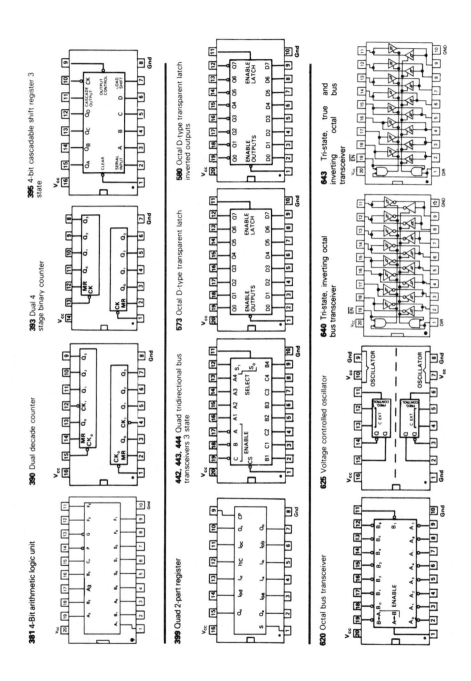

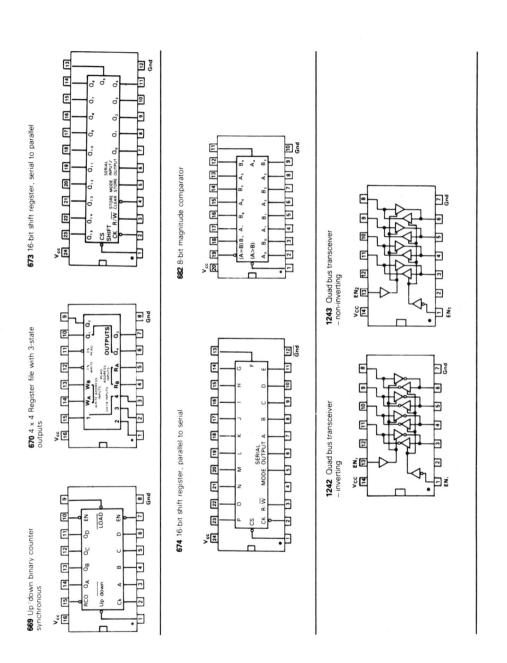

669 Up / down binary counter synchronous

670 4 x 4 Register file with 3-state outputs

673 16-bit shift register, serial to parallel

674 16-bit shift register, parallel to serial

682 8-bit magnitude comparator

1242 Quad bus transceiver – inverting

1243 Quad bus transceiver – non-inverting

Appendix C: ASCII Character Set

Character	Hex	Character	Hex	Character	Hex
NUL	00	0	30		60
SOH	01	1	31	a	61
STX	02	2	32	b	62
ETX	03	3	33	c	63
EOT	04	4	34	d	64
ENQ	05	5	35	e	65
ACK	06	6	36	f	66
BEL	07	7	37	g	67
BS	08	8	38	h	68
HT	09	9	39	i	69
LF	0A	:	3A	j	6A
VT	0B	;	3B	k	6B
FF	0C	<	3C	l	6C
CR	0D		3D	m	6D
S0	0E	>	3E	n	6E
S1	0F	?	3F	o	6F
DLE	10	@	40	p	70
DC1	11	A	41	q	71
DC2	12	B	42	r	72
DC3	13	C	43	s	73
DC4	14	D	44	t	74
NAK	15	E	45	u	75
SYN	16	F	46	v	76
ETB	17	G	47	w	77
CAN	18	H	48	x	78
EM	19	I	49	y	79
SUB	1A	J	4A	z	7A
ESC	1B	K	4B	{	7B
FS	1C	L	4C	¦	7C
GS	1D	M	4D	}	7D
RS	1E	N	4E	~	7E
US	1F	O	4F	DEL	7F

SP	20	P	50
!	21	Q	51
"	22	R	52
#	23	S	53
$	24	T	54
%	25	U	55
&	26	V	56
'	27	W	57
(	28	X	58
)	29	Y	59
*	2A	Z	5A
+	2B	[	5B
,	2C	\	5C
–	2D	]	5D
.	2E	^	5E
/	2F	–	5F

Note: Characters hex 00 to IF are control characters.
Character hex 7F is delete, or rub-out.

Glossary

Accumulator. A special *CPU register* that receives the results of most *ALU* operations.

ADC. *Analogue*-to-*digital* converter.

Address bus. The *microcomputer bus* that carries the *memory* address of the *instruction* that is being fetched, or a *data* item that is being transferred between the *CPU* and *memory* or *input/output*.

Address decoder. A circuit that generates *chip select* signals for each *memory* or *input/output* chip within a *microcomputer*.

Addressing mode. A method of specifying the location of a *data* item that is being accessed within an *instruction*.

ALU. Arithmetic and Logic Unit. The module within the *CPU* that performs arithmetic, for example add and subtract, and logic, for example *AND* and *OR* operations.

Analogue. A continuous signal that can take any value over its range.

AND. The *Boolean* logic function that generates logic 1 only if both comparison (or input) bits are also at logic 1.

Application program. A *program* in a *disk*-based *computer* that tailors the machine to a specific commercial/scientific function, for example word processor, spreadsheet, database, payroll.

ASCII. American Standard Code for Information Interchange. The code that is used to represent characters in *computers,* printers and *VDUs*.

ASIC. Application Specific Integrated Circuit. An *IC* that is designed to perform a single powerful function, for example a digital signal processor.

Assembler. A *program* that converts an *assembly language* program into *machine code*.

Assembly language. A programming language that is line-for-line convertible to *machine code,* but uses mnemonics for the *instruction* type ('opcode') and labels for *memory* addresses.

Audio cassette recorder. A domestic tape recorder that is used to store *microcomputer programs*.

Backing store. A bulk storage device, for example *floppy disk* or *hard disk,* for *programs* and *data* files.

BASIC. Beginners All-purpose Symbolic Instruction Code. The most popular *high-level language* that is used with *microcomputers*.

Baud rate. The speed of transmission of *serial data* expressed in bits/second.

BCD. Binary Coded Decimal. A 4-bit code that represents the numbers 0 to 9.

Binary. A number system that uses the base of 2. The only symbols used in binary numbers are 0 and 1.

Bistable. Two-state. A 'bistable multivibrator', or 'flip–flop', holds either logic 0 or logic 1.

Bit. Binary digit. A bit has two states – 0 and 1.

Boolean logic. A collection of logic functions named after George Boole. The Boolean logic functions *AND, OR* and *Exclusive-OR* are applied by software on binary numbers in *computers*.

Bootstrap. A *program* that loads the main program (normally the *'operating system,')* from *backing store* into *memory* when the *computer* is switched on.

Bounce. Unwanted repeated operation of a mechanical contact.

Branch. As for *jump*.

Breakpoint. A stop that is inserted into a *program* to assist in the testing of a new or faulty program.

Buffer. A temporary storage *register*.

Bug. A *software* error.

Burst memory transfer. A continuous *DMA* transfer.

Bus. A set of signal connections that have a common function. A *microcomputer* possesses an *address bus, data bus* and control bus.

Byte. Eight *bits*.

Cache. A fast *memory* circuit that is placed between the *CPU* (or on the CPU) and its memory circuit (normally *dynamic RAM*). It stores the most frequently addressed locations.

Call. An *instruction* that transfers *program* control to a *subroutine*.

Carry flag. A *bit* in a *CPU status register* which indicates that the result of an *ALU* operation has exceeded the number range of the ALU.

Central Processor Unit. See *CPU*.

Centronics interface. The international standard for the signal interface between a *computer* and a parallel-drive printer.

Checksum. A number that is placed after a list of *data* values in order to provide a means of confirming that the data list is read correctly.

Chequerboard pattern. An alternating *bit* pattern of 101010, etc., used to test various *computer* devices.

Chip. A common name for an *integrated circuit*.

Chip carrier. An *IC* package that uses the four sides of the device for interconnecting pins – used for devices with a large number of interconnecting pins.

Chip select. A control signal that activates a *memory* or *input/output chip*.

CMOS. Complementary Metal Oxide Semiconductor. A family of *integrated circuits* that offers extremely high packing density and low power consumption.

Common bus. A set of interfacing connections that allows *microcomputer* boards to be interconnected. Examples are the Versabus, S-100 bus and VME bus.

Compiler. A *program* that converts a *high-level language* program into *machine code* before program run-time and stores both versions on *backing store*.

Complement. Change a *bit* from 1 to 0 or 0 to 1.

Computer. A programmable *data* processing system.

Concurrency. The execution of more than one function by a *computer* at the same time, for example parallel processing with more than one *CPU*.

Control register. The *register* in a programmable *input/output* device, for example *UART, PIO, CTC* or *FDC,* that is used to select the programmable options within the device.

Control unit. The module within the CPU that examines and implements the current *instruction*.

Counter/timer. See *CTC*.

CPU. Central Processor unit. The main *computer* module, which fetches and implements *program instructions*. Its main sub-modules are the *ALU* and *control unit*. In a *microcomputer,* the CPU normally forms a single *IC* and is called a *microprocessor*.

CRO. Cathode Ray Oscilloscope. An item of test equipment that displays signal waveforms on a CRT.

CTC. Counter/Timer Circuit. A programmable input/output circuit that can be used to generate timer *interrupt* pulses, generate time delays or count external pulses. A CTC is either contained within a *PIO* chip, or it constitutes a separate chip.

Current tracer. A hand-held item of test equipment that detects changing current levels by electromagnetic induction.

Cursor. A small area of light on a CRT screen (part of a *VDU*) at which characters which are entered by the operator will appear.

DAC. *Digital*-to-*analogue* converter.

Daisy-chain. A connection system in which signal connections are linked from one module to another.

Data. A general term that can describe numbers, characters or groups of *bits* suitable for processing by *computer program*.

Data bus. The *microcomputer bus* that carries *data* (and *program instructions*) between *CPU* and *memory* or *input/output*.

Debugger. A test *program* that is used to locate and eliminate errors (or bugs) in a program under development.

Denary. The decimal number system that uses a base of 10.

Diagnostic. A test *program* that exercises parts of the hardware configuration to confirm correct operation.

Digit. Each symbol in a number system, for example a *binary* digit can be 0 or 1.

Digital. Possessing discrete states. *Computers* operate using *binary* signals, that is possessing only two states.

DIL. Dual-in-line. The standard *IC* package, in which interconnecting pins are placed along the two long sides of the rectangular device.

Directory. A list of all the *filenames* in a *computer* with a *backing store*.

DMA. Direct Memory Access. *Data* transfer between *memory* and *input/output* without passing through the *CPU*.

Dot matrix. A method of constructing characters using an array of dots, for example CRT/*VDU* and printer.

DVM. Digital voltmeter. An item of test equipment that displays voltage, current and resistance readings numerically.

Dynamic RAM. *RAM* memory that requires a regular refresh operation to prevent corruption of stored *bit* pattern.

Editor. A *program* that allows the operator to enter or amend a text *file*.

EPROM. Erasable Programmable Read Only Memory. *ROM* that can be erased by exposure to ultra-violet light and then re-programmed.

Exception. An alternative name for *interrupt* used by some *microprocessor* manufacturers.

Exclusive-OR. The *Boolean* logic function that generates logic 1 only if both comparison *bits* are different.

FDC. Floppy Disk Controller. A programmable *input/output chip* that controls a *floppy disk* drive.

FET. Field Effect Transistor. The principal component in *MOS* and *CMOS* circuits.

Fetch. The first part in the *fetch–execute cycle* which is implemented when the *CPU* obeys an *instruction*.

Fetch–execute cycle, The basic cycle that is implemented by the *CPU* when it obeys an *instruction*. Firstly the instruction is fetched from *memory* and secondly it is examined by the *control unit* and executed.

File. A *program* or *data* module held on *backing store*.

Firmware. *Program* or *data* resident in *ROM*.

Flag. A *bit* that indicates a specific condition or event.

Floating point. A number representation system for large and fractional numbers – the number is split into mantissa and exponent.

Floppy disk. A *backing store* medium that employs flexible magnetic disks.

Flowchart. The diagrammatic representation of the operation of a *program*.

Format. To initialise a blank *floppy disk* (or *hard disk*).

Free-run. To allow the *kernel* of a computer circuit to run in test mode – the *CPU* is forced continually to obey a single instruction.

Gate. A *digital* circuit with more than one input, but only one output. Gates perform *Boolean* logic functions.

GPIB. General Purpose Interface Bus. An alternative name for the IEEE488 *common bus*.

Hard disk. A *backing store* medium that employs a non-removable hard disk. A hard disk is faster, more expensive and possesses larger storage capacity than a *floppy disk*. It is often called a 'Winchester' disk.

Hardware. The physical equipment in a *computer* (to be distinguished from *software*).

Hexadecimal. A number system that uses a base of 16. Its particular use is to represent long *binary* numbers in an abbreviated form.

High-level language. A programming language that is similar to spoken language. A high-level language *program* must be converted to *machine code* before it is executed in a *computer*.

Hit rate. The success rate of locating the contents of a *memory* location in a *cache*.

IC. *Integrated circuit.*

In-circuit emulator. A combined *hardware* and *software* system that is used in a *MDS* to test a new *microprocessor*-based product.

Initialise. To set up an *input/output chip*, for example a *PIO, UART, CTC* or *FDC*, to one of its programmable states.

Input port. A circuit that passes external *digital* signals (normally 8) into a *CPU*.

Input/output. The *hardware* within a *computer* that connects the computer to external *peripherals* and devices.

Instruction. A single operation performed by a *computer*. A *low-level language program* consists of a list of instructions.

Integrated circuit. A circuit package that contains several components built into the same semiconductor wafer. This silicon wafer is housed in either a *DIL* or *chip carrier*.

Interactive. The characteristic of a *program* that asks the operator questions during the implementation of the program.

Interface. The circuit and interconnection system between a *computer* and its external devices.

Interpreter. A *program* that converts a *high-level language* program into *machine code* at run-time, rather than prior to run-time (see *compiler*).

Interrupt. An external signal (part of the *CPU*'s control bus) that suspends a *program* operating within a *computer* and causes entry into a special interrupt program. The latter is normally named an *interrupt service routine*.

Interrupt service routine. A *program* that is entered following an *interrupt*.

Jump. An *instruction* that sends *program* control to a specified *memory* location.

K. A symbol that represents decimal 1024.

Kansas standard. A signal specification for *data* storage on *audio cassette recorders*.

Kernel. The central circuit within a *computer*, that is *CPU*, clock circuit, Reset circuit and any bus buffers.

Label. A name given to a *memory* location in an *assembly language program*.

Language. A prescribed set of characters and symbols which is used to convey a *program* to a *computer*. A programming language can be a *high-level language* or a *low-level language*.

Latch. A circuit that staticises *bits*.

LED. Light Emitting Diode. A diode that emits light when current passes through it. It is often used in a LED *segment display* unit or for single-bit indication.

Loader. A *program* that converts a 'printable' version of a *machine code program* into executable machine code.

Logic. The application of a range of circuit building blocks to perform switching and control functions.

Logic analyser. An item of test equipment used for testing *digital* electronic systems, for example *computers*. A *CRT* is used to display information recorded from the system under test.

Logic comparator. A test board that monitors a *digital IC* and indicates if it produces different output signals to a reference IC.

Logic level. The voltage value that is used to indicate logic 0 or 1. For *TTL* and TTL-compatible circuits (including most *microprocessors* and their support *chips*) logic 0 = 0 V, and logic 1 = +5 V.

Logic monitor. A clip that is placed over a *digital IC* and indicates on *LEDs* the *logic* level at each pin.

Logic probe. A hand-held item of test equipment that indicates *logic* levels using *LEDs*.

Logic pulser. A hand-held item of test equipment that injects pulses into a system under test.

Loop. A section of *program* that is executed more than once.

Low-level language. A *computer* programming *language* that specifies each operation/instruction that the *CPU* is to perform. There are two classifications of low level language: *assembly language* and *machine code.*

M. A symbol that represents approximately a million (1 048 576). See also *K.*

Machine code. A *program* expressed in *binary* form, that is in the way in which it is executed within the *CPU.*

Mail. Messages that can be passed between users on a multi-user *computer* system.

Main memory. Fast *memory* which holds the *program* currently being executed. Main memory can be *ROM, RAM* or a mixture of the two.

Mainframe computer. A large multi-user *computer* with high processing power and a wide range of *peripherals.* Typical applications are for payroll, large customer accounts systems, large database applications.

Matrix printer. A printer that constructs characters using a dot matrix.

MDS. Microprocessor Development System. A *computer* that is used to develop *software* for prototype *microcomputer* applications.

Memory. Any circuit or *peripheral* that staticises *data.* Normally the term is used in place of *main memory.*

Memory management. A circuit (sometimes part of the *CPU* in the case of 32-*bit microprocessors*) that can modify the address generated by the CPU.

Memory map. A diagrammatic representation of the organisation of the *memory* range of a *computer.*

Memory mapped input/output. *Input/output* devices that are treated by *hardware* and *software* as *memory* devices.

Microcomputer. A complete *computer* on a handful of *integrated circuits* (or even a single integrated circuit). *VLSI* components are used for *CPU, memory* and *input/output.*

Microprocessor. A *CPU* constructed on a single *VLSI integrated circuit.*

Minicomputer. An arbitrary name given to a multi-user *computer* that performs down-market applications to a *mainframe computer.* Minicomputers are used extensively for industrial control applications. They are normally 16-*bit* machines.

Mnemonic. A group of letters (or symbols) that is used to represent the function of an *instruction* expressed in *assembly language* form.

Modem. An item of equipment that converts *logic* levels to frequencies, and vice versa. It is used for *serial* communication systems that pass through the public telephone network.

Monitor. The main *program* in some *microcomputers.*

MOS. Metal Oxide Semiconductor. A family of *integrated circuits* that offers high packing density (*VLSI*). Most *microprocessors* and their supporting *memory* and *input/output chips* are constructed using MOS technology.

Multiplexing. The technique of passing more than one signal along a single conductor.

Nesting. A *program loop* within another loop. Alternatively a *subroutine* within another subroutine.

NOP. No-operation. A *program instruction* that performs no processing, but simply uses some *CPU* time.

Nybble. 4 *bits.*

Object code. The name given to a *machine code* version of a *program.* The term is used to distinguish this version from the *source program,* which is *assembly language* or *high-level language.*

Opcode. The part of a *machine code instruction* that specifies the function of the instruction, for example add, shift, *jump.*

Operand. The part of a *machine code instruction* that specifies the *data* value or its *memory* address.

Operating system. The main *program* in a *disk*-based *computer.*

OR. The *Boolean logic* function that generates logic 1 if either of the comparison (or input) *bits* is set to logic 1.

Output port. A circuit that passes *digital* signals (normally a group of 8 parallel *bits*) outside a *microcomputer.*

Parity. The number, expressed as odd or even, of *logic* 1s in a *data* value.

Pascal. A *high-level language.*

PCB. Printed Circuit Board. A conventional circuit board with etched copper track interconnections between components.

Peripheral. An item of equipment that is external to a *computer,* for example printer, *VDU, floppy disk.*

PIO. Parallel Input/Output. A programmable multi-*port input/output chip.*

Pipeline. A small storage area within some *CPUs* that hold the next few *instructions* to be obeyed – the instructions are read out of *memory* before they are required in order to increase *program* execution speed.

Pixel. A dot position on a *CRT* screen.

PLA. Programmable Logic Array. An *IC* that consists of an array of *logic* gates that can be programmed to perform an overall logic function by the operator.

Poll. Regularly to check the status of an external signal or device by *software.*

Port. An input or output parallel-connection channel between a *computer* and external equipment. Normally a port is 8-*bits* wide.

Program. A set of processing steps that a *computer's CPU* is required to perform.

Program counter. A *CPU register* that holds the address in *memory* of the next *instruction* to be obeyed.

PROM. Programmable Read Only Memory. *ROM* that is programmed after the *chip* is manufactured. Once programmed it cannot be altered.

Pseudo-instruction. An *instruction* in an *assembly language program* that acts as a command to the *assembler* and is not converted to *machine code*.

RAM. Random Access Memory. RAM is semiconductor read/write *memory*. It is misnamed because *ROM* is also random access. There are two classifications of RAM: *static RAM* and *dynamic RAM*.

Read. To transfer *data* from *memory* to the *CPU*.

Refresh. To reinstate *data* in *dynamic RAM* or displayed on a *segment display* or CRT.

Register. A storage device for several *bits*. A *microprocessor* contains several work registers, as well as special-function registers.

Return. An *instruction* that returns *program* control to a main program from a *subroutine* or *interrupt service routine*.

RISC. Reduced Instruction Set Computer. A *CPU* that possesses only a limited *instruction* set in order to achieve high-speed performance. An example is the *transputer*.

ROM. Read Only Memory. ROM is semiconductor *memory* which can only be read from. There are three classifications of ROM: ROM (bit pattern stored is set when *chip* is manufactured), *PROM* and *EPROM*.

RS232-C. The internationally recognised specification for *serial data* transfer between *computers* and serial-drive *peripherals* (or other computers).

SBC. Single Board Computer.

Segment. An area of *memory* – typically 64*K* in several 16-*bit microprocessor* systems.

Segment display. A display that constructs numbers and letters by a network of segments.

Semiconductor memory. *ROM* and *RAM*.

Serial. The transfer of *data* items by setting one *bit* at a time on a single conductor.

Shift. Transfer of *data* to the left or right (normally within a *register*).

Software. *Computer programs* and *data files*.

Source program. The name given to an *assembly language* or *high-level language* version of a *program*.

Stack. A reserved area of *memory* (must be *RAM*) that is used by most *microprocessors* to store the return address in *subroutines* and *interrupt service routines*.

Static RAM. Conventional *RAM*, unlike *dynamic RAM* which requires refreshing.

Static stimulus tester (SST). A device that is used to test a *microcomputer* board. The *CPU* is removed from the board under test and signals from the SST are injected into the CPU's bus connections in order to test *memory* and *input/output* devices.

Status register. A collection of *flag bits* in a *microprocessor* that indicates the state of the *ALU*.

Subroutine. A section of *program* that is separated from the main program, but can be called several times from the main program.

SUT. System Under Test.

System program. The *operating system* or a utility *program* that supports the operating system, for example *editor, compiler, assembler*.

Tag address. The address of a *memory* location that is held in a *cache*.

Transputer. A *microprocessor* family produced by Inmos. Transputer arrays are designed to perform the *CPU* function in high-speed *computer* systems.

Tristate. A circuit in which its outputs can be set into one of three states: logic 0, logic 1 or 'floating' (high impedance, that is electrically isolated).

TTL. Transistor Transistor Logic. A family of *integrated circuits* that preceded *MOS* and *CMOS*, but is still widely used for *gates*, buffers, flip–flops (*bistables*), etc.

TTY. Teletype. A name sometimes given to a printer

Two's complement. A *binary* numbering system used to represent both positive and negative numbers – the most significant *bit* acts as a sign bit.

UART. Universal Asynchronous Receiver Transmitter. An *input/output* *chip* that handles *serial data* transfer, for example to *VDU*, printer or other *computer*. The *RS232-C* interface is generated by the device.

Utility program. A *program* that supports an *operating system*, for example a *compiler, editor, assembler*, etc.

VDU. Visual Display Unit. An operator device that includes a *CRT* for display purposes and a keyboard for manual entry. It is invariably connected to a *computer* by *serial RS232-C* link.

Vector. Part (or all) of a *memory* address that contains the start address of an *interrupt service routine*.

VLSI. Very Large Scale Integration. A measure of the packing density of an *integrated circuit* (more than 1000 *gates* per *chip*). Used as a description of *MOS* and *CMOS* devices.

Volatile memory. *Memory* that loses its stored *bit* pattern when power is removed.

VRAM. Video RAM. *RAM* that is used to store video *data*.

Winchester. Another name for a *hard disk*.

Word. A unit of *data* in a *computer*. The word length is the same as the *bit* length of the *CPU,* for example *microprocessors* are expressed as 8-bit, 16-bit or 32-bit devices.

Word processor. A *program* that is used to create and amend text *files*, for example letters, reports, *source programs*.

Write. To transfer *data* to *memory* from the *CPU*.

Write protect. To set a *backing store* device to read-only to protect against *file* over-writing.

Index